PowerPoint 2002:
Basic

Student Manual

COURSE TECHNOLOGY

Australia • Canada • Mexico • Singapore
Spain • United Kingdom • United States

PowerPoint 2002: Basic

VP and GM of Courseware:	Michael Springer
Series Product Managers:	Caryl Bahner-Guhin, Charles G. Blum, and Adam A. Wilcox
Production Editor:	Karen Jacot
Project Editor:	Debbie Masi
Key Tester:	Laurie Perry
Series Designer:	Adam A. Wilcox
Cover Designer:	Steve Deschene

For more information contact:

Course Technology
25 Thomson Place
Boston, MA 02210

Or find us on the Web at: www.course.com

For permission to use material from this text or product, contact us by

• Web: www.thomsonrights.com
• Phone: 1-800-730-2214
• Fax: 1-800-730-2215

Trademarks

Course ILT is a trademark of Course Technology.

Some of the product names and company names used in this book have been used for identification purposes only and may be trademarks or registered trademarks of their respective manufacturers and sellers.

Disclaimer

Course Technology reserves the right to revise this publication and make changes from time to time in its content without notice.

ISBN 0-619-07437-X

Printed in Canada

6 7 8 9 10 PM 06 05 04 03

Contents

PowerPoint 2002: Basic

Introduction

After reading this introduction, you'll know how to:

A Use Course Technology ILT manuals in general.

B Use prerequisites, a target student description, course objectives, and a skills inventory to properly set your expectations for the course.

C Re-key this course after class.

Topic A: About the manual

Course Technology ILT philosophy

Course Technology ILT manuals facilitate your learning by providing structured interaction with the software itself. While we provide text to explain difficult concepts, the hands-on activities are the focus of our courses. By paying close attention as your instructor leads you through these activities, you'll learn the skills and concepts effectively.

We believe strongly in the instructor-led classroom. During class, focus on your instructor. Our manuals are designed and written to facilitate your interaction with your instructor, and not to call attention to manuals themselves.

We believe in the basic approach of setting expectations, delivering instruction, and providing summary and review afterwards. For this reason, lessons begin with objectives and end with summaries. We also provide overall course objectives and a course summary to provide both an introduction to and closure on the entire course.

Manual components

The manuals contain these major components:

- Table of contents
- Introduction
- Units
- Course summary
- Reference
- Index

Each element is described below.

Table of contents

The table of contents acts as a learning roadmap.

Introduction

The introduction contains information about our training philosophy and our manual components, features, and conventions. It contains target student, prerequisite, objective, and setup information for the specific course.

Units

Units are the largest structural component of the course content. A unit begins with a title page that lists objectives for each major subdivision, or topic, within the unit. Within each topic, conceptual and explanatory information alternates with hands-on activities. Units conclude with a summary comprising one paragraph for each topic, and an independent practice activity that gives you an opportunity to practice the skills you've learned.

The conceptual information takes the form of text paragraphs, exhibits, lists, and tables. The activities are structured in two columns, one telling you what to do, the other providing explanations, descriptions, and graphics.

Course summary

This section provides a text summary of the entire course. It's useful for providing closure at the end of the course. The course summary also indicates the next course in this series, if there is one, and lists additional resources you might find useful as you continue to learn about the software.

Reference

The reference is an at-a-glance job aid summarizing some of the more common features of the software.

Index

The index enables you to quickly find information about a particular feature or concept of the software.

Manual conventions

We've tried to keep the number of elements and the types of formatting to a minimum in the manuals. This aids in clarity and makes the manuals more classically elegant looking. But there are some conventions and icons you should know about.

Convention/Icon	Description
Italic text	In conceptual text, indicates a new term or feature.
Bold text	In unit summaries, indicates a key term or concept. In an independent practice activity, indicates an explicit item that you select, choose, or type.
Code font	Indicates code or syntax.
Select **bold item**	In the left column of hands-on activities, bold sans-serif text indicates an explicit item that you select, choose, or type.
Keycaps like ⏎ ENTER	Indicate a key on the keyboard you must press.

Hands-on activities

The hands-on activities are the most important parts of our manuals. They're divided into two primary columns. The "Here's how" column gives short instructions to you about what to do. The "Here's why" column provides explanations, graphics, and clarifications. Here's a sample:

Do it!

A-1: Creating a commission formula

Here's how	Here's why
1 Open Sales	This is an oversimplified sales compensation worksheet. It shows sales totals, commissions, and incentives for five sales representatives.
2 Observe the contents of cell F4	F4 ▼ = =E4*C_Rate The commission rate formulas use the name "C_Rate" instead of a value for the commission rate.

For these activities, we provided a collection of data files designed to help you learn each skill in a real-world business context. As you work through the activities, you'll modify and update these files. Of course, you might make a mistake and, therefore, want to re-key the activity starting from scratch. To make it easy to start over, you'll rename each data file at the end of the first activity in which the file is modified. Our convention for renaming files is to add the word "My" to the beginning of the file name. In the above activity, for example, a file called "Sales" is used for the first time. At the end of this activity, you would save the file as "My sales," thus leaving the "Sales" file unchanged. If you make a mistake, you can start over by using the original "Sales" file.

In some activities, however, it might not be practical to rename the data file. If you want to retry one of these activities, ask your instructor for a fresh copy of the original data file.

Topic B: Setting your expectations

Properly setting your expectations is essential to your success. This topic will help you do that by providing:

- Prerequisites for this course
- A description of the target student at whom the course is aimed
- A list of the objectives for the course
- A skills assessment for the course

Course prerequisites

Before taking this course, you should be familiar with personal computers and the use of a keyboard and a mouse. Furthermore, this course assumes that you've completed the following courses or have equivalent experience:

- *Windows 95: Basic* or *Windows 98: Basic* or *Windows 2000: Basic* or *equivalent experience*

Target student

The target student for the course is an individual who wants to learn the basic features of PowerPoint to create effective presentations by using the drawing tools, clip art, WordArt, charts, and tables.

Course objectives

These overall course objectives will give you an idea about what to expect from the course. It's also possible that they will help you see that this course is not the right one for you. If you think you either lack the prerequisite knowledge or already know most of the subject matter to be covered, you should let your instructor know that you think you are misplaced in the class.

After completing this course, you'll know how to:

- Explore the PowerPoint environment and use Help options.
- Create a new presentation, add new slides to it, save and update changes, work in the Outline tab to rearrange bullets, rearrange and delete slides, and insert slides from another presentation.
- Use the Formatting toolbar, use the Cut, Copy, and Paste commands, examine the ruler, check spelling in a presentation, and use AutoCorrect and the Style Checker.
- Create objects by using the Drawing toolbar, add AutoShapes to a slide, draw text boxes, and edit AutoShapes.
- Use the WordArt toolbar to enhance text in a presentation, and insert and explore clip art on the Web.
- Add a table, use Microsoft Graph, and create an organization chart.
- Apply a design template, edit a slide master, work with multiple slide masters, add and delete slide masters, adjust the pace of a presentation, and add speaker notes and footers to each slide in a presentation.

- Hide a slide, print a presentation, export to Microsoft Word format, save a presentation for Web delivery, and add a link to another presentation.

Skills inventory

Use the following form to gauge your skill level upon entering the class. For each skill listed, rate your familiarity from 1 to 5, with five being the most familiar. *This is not a test*. Rather, it's intended to provide you with an idea of where you're starting from at the beginning of class. If you're entirely unfamiliar with all the skills, you might not be ready for the class. If you think you already understand all of the skills, you might need to move on to the next Module in the series. In either case, you should let your instructor know as soon as possible.

Skill	1	2	3	4	5
Start Microsoft PowerPoint	X				
Identify PowerPoint's views					
Open, save, and close presentations					
Rearrange, delete, and insert slides					
Change font type, size, and bullet style					
Use the Cut, Copy, and Paste commands					
View the ruler, set tabs, and align text					
Check spelling, use AutoCorrect and the Style Checker					
Create, move, and resize objects					
Work with AutoShapes and text boxes					
Enhance a presentation by using WordArt and clip art					
Add a table to a slide and enter text in it					
Create a chart, change its colors, and change the chart type					
Create an organization chart and add levels to it					
Apply design templates and use multiple slide masters					
Add transition effects and timings to a slide show					
Print presentations					
Export presentations to Microsoft Word					
Save presentations as Web pages					
Insert hyperlinks into a slide					

Topic C: Re-keying the course

If you have the proper hardware and software, you can re-key this course after class. This section explains what you'll need to do so, and how to do it.

Computer requirements

To re-key this course, your personal computer must have:

- A keyboard and a mouse
- PC with a Pentium 200 MHz processor or higher
- 64 MB RAM (128 MB recommended)
- 170 MB available hard disk space
- A 3½-inch floppy disk drive if you want to load the data files from disk
- SVGA monitor (800 x 600 minimum resolution support)
- CD-ROM drive
- A printer connection or, at the least, a printer driver.
- Sound card and speaker installed (This will be required if you need to complete all the activities in Unit 7.)
- Internet connection required to download student data files and to complete several Web-based activities, such as accessing help on the Web, Clips Online, and publishing a presentation to the Web.

Setup instructions to re-key the course

Before you re-key the course, you'll need to perform the following steps.

1   Install Microsoft Windows 2000 Professional Edition according to the software manufacture's instructions, if necessary.

2   Use the Internet Connection Wizard to establish an Internet connection.

3   Set the home page for Internet Explorer to about:blank. To do so, right-click the Internet Explorer icon on the desktop and choose Properties. On the General tab, enter "about:blank" as the home page address.

4   Install Microsoft Office XP. Select the Custom installation option, click Next. Clear all the check boxes except Microsoft PowerPoint, Microsoft Word, and Microsoft Excel. Then, select Choose detailed installation options for each application and click Next. Click the drop-down arrow next to Microsoft PowerPoint for Windows, and choose Run all from My Computer. Click Next and then, click Install to start the installation.

5 Start Microsoft PowerPoint. The Microsoft Office Professional with FrontPage Activation Wizard appears. Follow the on-screen instructions of the wizard to activate the software. Choose Help, Show the Office Assistant to display the Office Assistant, if necessary. Right-click Office Assistant and choose Options to open the Office Assistant dialog box. Clear the Use the Office Assistant check box and click OK. If necessary, drag the Formatting toolbar below the Standard toolbar. Choose Tools, Options, click the View tab, and verify that under Slide show, End with black slide is checked. Close Microsoft PowerPoint.

6 If necessary, reset any defaults that you changed. If you don't wish to reset the defaults, you can still re-key the course, but some activities might not work exactly as documented.

7 Create a folder called Student Data at the root of the hard drive.

8 Download the Student Data examples for the course (if you don't have an Internet connection, you can ask your instructor for a copy of the data files on a disk).

   a Connect to www.courseilt.com/instructor_tools.html.

   b Click the link for PowerPoint 2002 to display a page of course listings, and then click the link for PowerPoint 2002: Basic.

   c Click the link for downloading the data disk files, and follow the instructions that appear on your screen.

9 Copy the data files for the course to the Student Data folder.

Unit 1

PowerPoint 2002 basics

Unit time: 30 minutes

Complete this unit, and you'll know how to:

A Explore the PowerPoint environment.

B Use Help options.

C Close a presentation and close PowerPoint.

Topic A: Exploring the PowerPoint environment

Explanation

The *PowerPoint* program is included in the Microsoft Office suite. You can use PowerPoint to create presentations that combine text, graphics, charts, clip art, and Word Art. These presentations can then be shown at internal business meetings, sales calls, and training events. You can also show a PowerPoint presentation to a potential client or post it on either the Internet or a company intranet.

You can deliver presentations through various media, including timed shows on a computer, slides, overheads, printouts with notes, and on the Web.

Opening presentations

You can start PowerPoint by choosing Microsoft PowerPoint from the Start Programs menu.

To open an existing presentation:

1   Choose File, Open to display the Open dialog box.
2   From the Look in list, select the folder and file name of the presentation that you want to open.
3   Click Open.

You can also click the Open button on the Standard toolbar to access the Open dialog box.

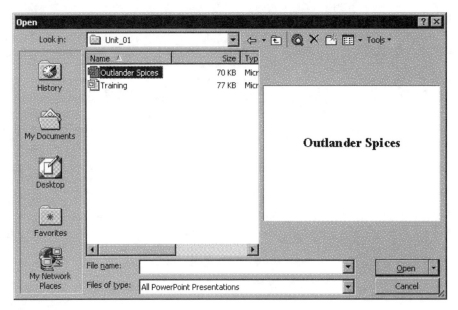

Exhibit 1-1: The Open dialog box

Running presentations

To display a presentation, you need to run a slide show. When you run a slide show, PowerPoint displays one slide at a time. You can advance the slides manually, or you can have PowerPoint advance the slides automatically. To move to the next slide in the show, you can either click the mouse or use the Page Down key. To move to the previous slide, right-click and choose Previous from the shortcut menu or use the Page Up key.

Do it!

A-1:   Opening and running a presentation

Here's how	Here's why
1 Choose **Start**, **Programs**, **Microsoft PowerPoint**	To start PowerPoint.
Observe the screen	You'll see the PowerPoint window, which contains a blank presentation.
2 Choose **File**, **Open…**	To display the Open dialog box.
3 From the Look in list, select **Student Data**	
Double-click the current unit folder	You'll see a list of presentations.
4 Select **Outlander Spices**	(If necessary.) You'll open this presentation. A preview of the presentation appears on the right side of the dialog box, as shown in Exhibit 1-1.
5 Click **Open**	To open the presentation. The first slide appears in the PowerPoint window.
6 Choose **Slide Show**, **View Show**	(To start the slide show.) A black screen appears for a while with the text, "Starting slide show."
Observe the first slide	You'll see the title slide.
7 Click the mouse	To move to the next slide.
Observe the slide	You'll see the bulleted slide titled "Project justification."
8 Click the mouse	To see a slide with formatted text.
9 Move to the next slide	(Click the mouse.) This is the fourth slide; it contains drawing objects.
10 Move to the next slide	To see the fifth slide containing clip art and WordArt.

11	Press PAGE UP	To move to the previous slide. You can use the Page Up and Page Down keys to navigate through the slide show.
12	Press PAGE DOWN	To move to the next slide. This is the fifth slide.
13	Press PAGE DOWN	To see a slide containing a table.
14	Move to the next slide	To see a slide containing an organization chart.
15	Move to the next slide	The slide show ends. You'll see a black screen.
16	Click the mouse	To exit the show and return to the first slide.

Examining the PowerPoint environment

Explanation   The PowerPoint window contains elements that are common to Windows applications.

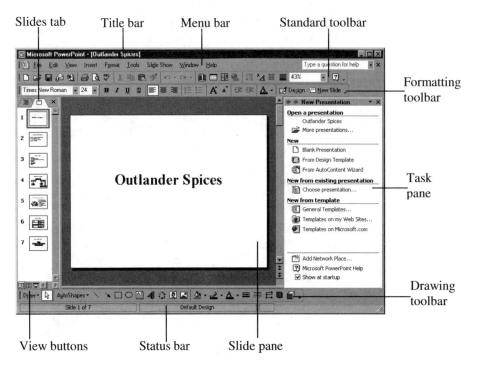

Exhibit 1-2: The PowerPoint window

The following table explains some components of the PowerPoint window:

Component	Description
Title bar	Displays the name of the application and the name of the presentation file.
Menu bar	Provides menus so that you can communicate with PowerPoint. Each menu has a set of commands of a certain type. For example, the Edit menu contains commands to edit text.
Toolbars	The buttons on a toolbar enable you to perform common tasks by clicking a button instead of using a menu command. By default, PowerPoint displays the Standard, Formatting, and Drawing toolbars. Toolbar buttons for the most commonly used tasks are displayed.
Status bar	Located at the bottom of the PowerPoint window. It displays information such as the slide number and the name of the design template that you selected.
View buttons	Located in the lower-left corner of the PowerPoint window, above the Drawing toolbar. You can use these buttons to display slides in any of the three PowerPoint views.

Task panes

PowerPoint 2002 provides several task panes that help you work easily with your files. Some commonly used task panes are the New Presentation task pane, the Slide Layout task pane, and the Slide Transition task pane. These task panes are small in size and are located on the right side of the PowerPoint window. To use these task panes, you need to display them. For example, to display the New Presentation task pane, you can choose File, New. This task pane provides many commands that you can use to create a new presentation, such as New, New from existing presentation, and New from template.

Do it!

A-2:   Examining the PowerPoint environment

Here's how	Here's why
1 Choose **View**, **Task Pane**	(If necessary.) To display the task pane.
2 Observe the window title bar	You'll see the name of the presentation file, "Outlander Spices."
3 Observe the menu bar	The menu bar provides options you can use to work with PowerPoint.
4 Observe the toolbars	You'll see the Standard, Formatting, and Drawing toolbars.
5 Observe the Slides tab	This tab is on the left side of the PowerPoint window. It displays all the slides of the presentation as thumbnails.

6 Observe the Slide pane	This is the middle pane of the PowerPoint window. It displays the slide.
7 Observe the task pane	You can use it to access commonly used commands easily.
8 Observe the status bar	The slide number of the current slide appears on the left side of the status bar.
9 Observe the view buttons	There are three view buttons that you can use to switch between different views.

Observing views

Explanation

PowerPoint has three views: Normal, Slide Sorter, and Slide Show. You can change between views by clicking the appropriate button.

View	Description
Normal view	Contains two tabs on the left and a slide pane on the right. The two tabs on the left are Outline and Slides. You can use the Outline tab to organize and develop the content of the presentation. The Slides tab shows your slides as thumbnails. You can use the Slide pane on the right to see how the text on each slide looks.
Slide Sorter view	Lets you see all the slides in the presentation at the same time, shown in miniature. You can arrange the order of the slides by using this view.
Slide Show	Lets you see your presentation on the full screen. Any special effects you add to your presentation, such as transitions and timings, are visible during the slide show.

Do it!   **A-3:   Observing views**

Here's how	**Here's why**
1 Click as shown	Times New Roman / Outline \ **Slides** / 1
	(On the left side of the window.) To display the Outline tab.

Observe the Outline tab	**Outline** \ Slides
	1 ▦ **Outlander Spices**
	2 ▦ **Project justification**
	   • Control inventory costs and levels
	   • Provide quality products
	   • Price products competitively
	   • Control cash flow

	You'll see an outline of all the text in the presentation.
2 Click the **Slides** tab	To return to the Slides tab.
3 Click ▦	To switch to Slide Sorter view. You'll see all the slides in the presentation. You can use this view to rearrange the order of the slides.
4 Click ▣	To run the slide show. You'll see the first slide of your presentation displayed on the full screen. You can also choose Slide Show, View Show to run the slide show.
5 Press (ESC)	To end the slide show.
6 Click ▣	To switch to Normal view.

Topic B: Help options

Explanation

You can use PowerPoint's Help system to get assistance while you work. You can access help by choosing Help, Microsoft PowerPoint Help, by pressing F1 on the keyboard, by using the Ask a Question box, or by using the Office Assistant. You can also get help from Microsoft through the Web. The Help window can be left open while you work in PowerPoint.

Using the Office Assistant

The Office Assistant is an animated help system that can answer your questions while you work. The Assistant lets you type questions and then displays appropriate help topics. If you don't find information related to the topic you want, the Assistant gives you suggestions as to how to phrase your question. To show the Office Assistant, choose Help, Show the Office Assistant. To hide it, choose Help, Hide the Office Assistant.

To find help in PowerPoint by using the Office Assistant:

1   Click the Office Assistant.
2   In the "What would you like to do?" balloon, type a few words about what you want to do. The Office Assistant lets you type questions in plain language.
3   Click Search.

Exhibit 1-3: The Office Assistant

Do it!

B-1:   Using the Office Assistant

Here's how	Here's why
1 Choose **Help, Show the Office Assistant**	You'll see the Office Assistant.
2 Click the Office Assistant	The "What would you like to do?" balloon appears on the screen. The balloon contains a text box in which you can type a question.
3 In the Office Assistant text box, type **open**	
Click **Search**	To display the Help topics that deal with opening files. You'll see several options.
4 Click **Open a file**	(To display the Help topic.) On the right side, you'll see a Help window that explains how to open a file.

5 Click **Options**	(In the Assistant balloon.) To display the Office Assistant dialog box.
6 Clear **Use the Office Assistant**	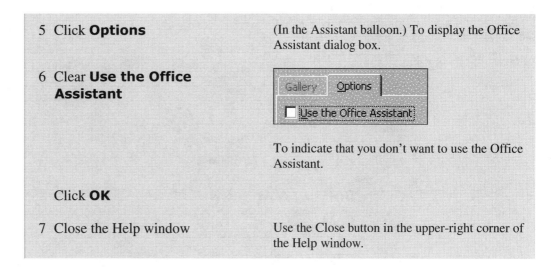
	To indicate that you don't want to use the Office Assistant.
Click **OK**	
7 Close the Help window	Use the Close button in the upper-right corner of the Help window.

The Ask a Question box

Explanation

You can use the Ask a Question box on the menu bar to access help quickly. You type a question in this box and then press Enter. PowerPoint help displays the answer or a list of possible answers.

Do it!

B-2: Using the Ask a Question box

Here's how	Here's why
1 In the Ask a Question box, enter **What is a task pane?**	What is a task pane? ▼ ✕
	The Ask a Question box is on the right side of the menu bar.
Observe the screen	A list of topics related to the task pane appears.
2 Click **See More...**	To display additional topics.
Click **Navigation and display of task panes**	To display help on this topic.
Observe the screen	On the right side, you'll see a Help window that explains about the task panes.
3 Close the Help window	

Help on the Web

Explanation

You can connect to the Microsoft Office Update Web site directly from PowerPoint. You can access technical information and download product enhancements. If you are using the Office Assistant or the Ask a Question box and you can't find the information you need, you have the option of connecting to the Web to find additional information.

To get help on the Web, choose Help, Office on the Web. This opens Internet Explorer and displays the Microsoft Office Update page. From this page, select a topic about which you want further information.

Do it!

B-3: Getting help on the Web

Here's how	Here's why
1 Choose **Help, Office on the Web**	To get help from the Web. This opens Internet Explorer and the Microsoft Office Update Web page.
2 Click **United States**	(On the map.) To get information on PowerPoint enhancements.
3 Close the browser window	

Topic C: Closing presentations and closing PowerPoint

Explanation

There are several ways to close a PowerPoint presentation:

- Choose File, Close.
- Click the Close button in the upper-right corner of the menu bar (as shown in Exhibit 1-4).
- Double-click the Control menu icon in the upper-left corner of the menu bar (also shown in Exhibit 1-4).
- Click the Control menu and choose Close.

Control menu   Close button

Exhibit 1-4: The Control menu icon and the Close button

Closing PowerPoint

There also are several ways to close the PowerPoint program:

- Choose File, Exit.
- Click the Close button in the upper-right corner of the title bar.
- Double-click the Control menu icon in the upper-left corner of the title bar.
- Press Alt+F4.

Do it!

C-1: Closing a presentation and closing PowerPoint

Here's how	Here's why
1 Choose **File**, **Close**	To close the presentation.
2 Choose **File**, **Exit**	To close PowerPoint.

Unit summary: PowerPoint 2002 basics

Topic A In this unit, you learned how to **open** and run a **PowerPoint presentation**. You examined the PowerPoint environment and saw the various components of the PowerPoint window, including **toolbars, menus** and **the task pane**. You learned about the various **views** PowerPoint provides.

Topic B Next, you learned about PowerPoint's various **help features**, including the **Office Assistant** and **Ask a Question box**. Then, you saw how to find information and help by using the **Web**.

Topic C Finally, you learned several ways to **close** a presentation and to **close** PowerPoint.

Independent practice activity

1 Start PowerPoint.

2 Open Training (from the current unit folder within the Student Data folder).

3 Switch to Slide Sorter view.

4 Switch to Slide Show view.

5 View the entire presentation.

6 Close the presentation (you don't need to save changes).

Unit 2

Building new presentations

Unit time: 45 minutes

Complete this unit, and you'll know how to:

A Create a new PowerPoint presentation and add slides to it.

B Save a presentation and update the changes made to it.

C Work in the Outline tab to rearrange bullet items.

D Rearrange and delete slides in the Outline tab and Slide Sorter view.

E Insert an existing slide into another presentation.

Topic A: Creating new presentations

Explanation

When you create a presentation in PowerPoint 2002, you can select a presentation type from three options: Blank Presentation, Design Template, and AutoContent Wizard. You can add slides with different layouts to your presentation. You can work in the Outline tab of Normal view to organize information in a slide or in an entire presentation. After you create your presentation, you can also save, make changes, and update it.

Creating presentations

To create a new presentation in PowerPoint 2002, choose File, New. The task pane displays three presentation options, as shown in Exhibit 2-1, that you can use to create a new presentation:

- *Blank Presentation:* Creates a new presentation with default settings for text and colors.
- *From Design Template:* Provides a collection of templates that you can apply to your presentation to specify how it will look.
- *From AutoContent Wizard:* Creates a presentation based on the content, purpose, style, handouts, and output you provide. You can replace the AutoContent Wizard sample text with your own text.

Exhibit 2-1: The new presentation options in the task pane

Slide layouts

After you select a blank presentation or a template to create your presentation, by default, PowerPoint adds a slide with the Title Slide layout in your presentation. However, you can select a different layout for your slides from the task pane, as shown in Exhibit 2-2. These layouts are categorized into: Text Layouts, Content Layouts, Text and Contents Layouts, and Other Layouts. These categories provide 27 *layout*s or formats for slides.

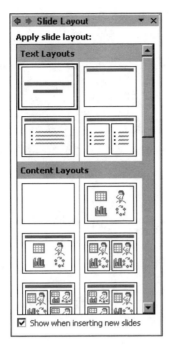

Exhibit 2-2: The Slide Layout task pane

Do it!

A-1:   Creating a new presentation from a blank presentation

Here's how	Here's why
1 Choose **File, New...**	(To create a new PowerPoint presentation.) The New Presentation task pane appears.
2 Under New, click **Blank Presentation**	 **New** ☐ Blank Presentation ▥ From Design Template ▣ From AutoContent Wizard (In the New Presentation task pane.) You'll create a blank presentation. The Slide Layout task pane appears.
Observe the Slide Layout task pane	It displays various slide layouts. By default, the first Text Layout is selected.

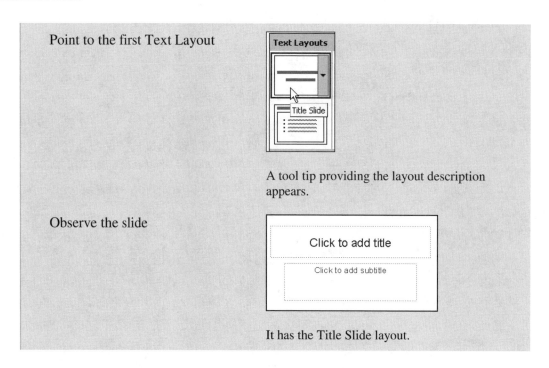

Point to the first Text Layout

A tool tip providing the layout description appears.

Observe the slide

It has the Title Slide layout.

Entering text in slides

Explanation

After you select a slide layout, you can enter text for the slide. The Title Slide layout contains two placeholders for text. The first is the title placeholder and the second is the subtitle placeholder.

The slide master

The title and text objects are formatted on a *slide master* to ensure that text for the entire presentation is formatted consistently. A slide master is a special slide that controls text formatting, background color, and special effects, such as shadowing and bullets.

Do it!

A-2: Entering text in a slide

Here's how	Here's why
1 Click the title placeholder	(On the slide.) To display the insertion point in the title placeholder.
2 Type **Outlander Spices**	This will be the slide's title.
3 Click the subtitle placeholder	To display the insertion point.
Type **Expansion project**	
4 Click anywhere outside the placeholder	To deselect it.

Adding new slides

Explanation   You can add a new slide to a presentation by choosing Insert, New Slide; by clicking the New Slide button on the Standard toolbar; or, by pressing Ctrl+M. Performing any of these actions adds a new slide in the presentation and displays the Slide Layout task pane. You can then select a layout for the new slide from this task pane.

Adding bullet slides

The Slide Layout task pane provides several layouts for adding bullet slides to a presentation, as shown in Exhibit 2-3. The Title and Text slide has two placeholders, one for the title and a second for the bullet list.

To insert text in the bullet-list placeholder:

1   Click the bullet-list placeholder.
2   Type the text for the first bullet.
3   Press Enter to display a second bullet.
4   Type the text for the second bullet and press Enter.
5   Continue this process to add text for additional bullets.
6   After entering the required number of bulleted items, click outside the placeholder to deselect it.

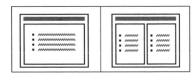

Exhibit 2-3: Some layouts for bullet slides

Do it!   ## A-3:   Adding a bullet slide

Here's how	Here's why
1 Click the New Slide button	New Slide
	On the Formatting toolbar.
Observe the selected layout in the Slide Layout task pane	
	Note that under Text Layouts, Title and Text layout is selected because it's a logical choice after a title slide.

Observe the slide	
	It has two placeholders, one of the slide's title and another for the bullet list.
Observe the Slides tab on the left	It shows that the presentation has two slides.
2 Click the title placeholder	To position the insertion point.
Type **Outlander Spices**	This will be the slide's title.
3 Click the bullet-list placeholder	To position the insertion point for the first bullet item.
4 Type **Project justification**	To create the first bullet item.
Press (↵ ENTER)	To add a second bullet.
5 Type **Performance**	In the second bullet displayed.
Observe the slide	It contains a title and a bulleted list with two items.

The AutoContent Wizard

Explanation

PowerPoint's AutoContent Wizard is useful when you need help in organizing a presentation. First, it provides several categories of presentation types from which you can choose, such as Projects or Sales/Marketing. Next, it prompts you to choose a method for delivering the presentation, such as on-screen, via the Web, or via overhead transparencies. Then it prompts you for the title of the first slide and an opportunity to add footer information.

When you complete the final Wizard step, PowerPoint creates a presentation based on your choices. The slides will include suggestions for both the content and organization of your presentation. You can use the provided text or replace it with your own.

To create a presentation by using the AutoContent Wizard:

1 Choose File, New to display the New Presentation task pane.

2 In the task pane, under New, click From AutoContent Wizard to open the AutoContent Wizard dialog box, and click Next.

3 Select an appropriate presentation category and click Next.

4 Select an appropriate presentation style and click Next.

5 In the Presentation title box, enter the presentation title. In the Footer box, enter the footer, if required. Select other appropriate presentation options, if required and click Next.

6 Click Finish to complete the presentation.

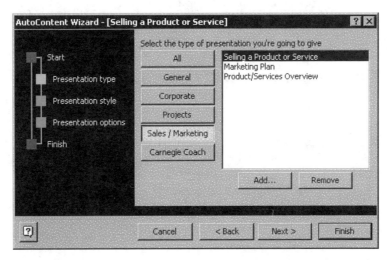

Exhibit 2-4: The second step of the AutoContent Wizard

Do it!

A-4:   Using the AutoContent Wizard

Here's how	Here's why
1 Choose **File**, **New...**	The New Presentation task pane is available.
2 Under New, click **From AutoContent Wizard**	
	(To start the wizard.) The introductory screen of the wizard appears.
3 Click **Next**	To advance to the next screen.
4 Click **Sales/Marketing**	(As shown in Exhibit 2-4.) To view the presentation types available in this category.
From the list, select **Marketing Plan**	
Click **Next**	A variety of presentation styles, such as On-screen presentation, Web presentation, Black and white overheads, and Color overheads appear.
5 Verify that On-screen presentation is selected	You'll deliver this presentation on-screen.
Click **Next**	

6	Under Presentation title, enter **New markets**	This title will appear on the Title slide.
	Observe the options under Items to include on each slide	If required, you can add a footer to each slide and include the date and a slide number.
7	Click **Next**	
	Click **Finish**	To complete the wizard and create the presentation.
8	Observe the Outline tab on the left	The presentation contains several slides, each of which contains suggested content.
	Press ⌷PAGE DOWN⌷	To view the next slide.

Topic B: Saving presentations

Explanation

You need to save your presentations to prevent data loss. You can use existing folders or create your own folders to save your presentations. You can also update your presentation to save the changes.

Saving presentations in existing folders

The first time you save a presentation, you must assign a file name and select a location or folder in which to store the file.

To save a presentation in an existing folder:

1   Choose File, Save As to display the Save As dialog box, as shown in Exhibit 2-5.
2   From the Save in list, select the drive and folder where you want to save the presentation.
3   In the File name box, type a name for the presentation.
4   Click Save.

Exhibit 2-5: A sample Save As dialog box

Do it!

B-1: Saving a presentation in an existing folder

Here's how	Here's why
1 Choose **File**, **Save As...**	To display the Save As dialog box.
2 From the Save in list, select **Student Data**	You'll select a folder to save your presentation.
3 Double-click the current unit folder	(From the Student Data folder.) You'll save the presentation in this folder.
4 Edit the File name box to read **Market report**	This will be the new presentation name.
Observe the Save as type box	By default, PowerPoint shows the type as Presentation.
Click **Save**	To save the presentation.
Observe the title bar	**Microsoft PowerPoint - [Market report]**
	You'll see that the file name appears in the title bar.
5 Choose **File**, **Close**	To close the presentation.

Saving presentations in new folders

Explanation

To save a presentation in a new folder:

1 Choose File, Save As to display the Save As dialog box.
2 Click the Create New Folder button to display the New Folder dialog box.
3 In the Name box, specify an appropriate folder name and click OK.
4 Verify that the Save in list displays the name of the newly created folder.
5 In the File name box, type a name for the presentation.
6 Click Save.

Do it!

B-2: Saving a presentation in a new folder

Here's how	Here's why
1 Choose **File**, **Save As...**	To display the Save As dialog box.
2 From the Save in list, select **Student Data**	You'll create a folder within the Student Data folder to save your presentation.
3 Click [icon]	(The Create New Folder button is in the Save As dialog box.) The New Folder dialog box appears.

4	In the Name box, enter **My folder**	This will be the folder's name.
	Click **OK**	Note that in the Save in list, My folder is selected.
5	Edit the File name box to read **My first presentation**	
6	Click **Save**	To save the presentation in the folder as My folder.

Updating presentations

Explanation

Each time you save a presentation, PowerPoint updates the file with your latest changes. To update the presentation, you can either choose File, Save or click the Save button on the Standard toolbar. You can also update changes by using the shortcut key Ctrl+S.

To save a copy of a presentation with a different name or in a different location, you use the Save As command.

Do it!

B-3:   Updating a presentation

Here's how	Here's why
1 Verify that the insertion point is at the end of the second bullet	You'll add more bullet items to the slide.
2 Press (↵ ENTER)	To add a bullet to the slide.
3 Type **Progress-to-date**	
Press (↵ ENTER)	
4 Type **Outstanding issues**	
Click outside the bullet placeholder	To deselect it.
Observe the slide	Outlander Spices • Project justification • Performance • Progress-to-date • Outstanding issues It should look like this.
5 Click 💾	(On the Standard toolbar.) To update the changes made to the presentation.
6 Close the presentation	Choose File, Close.

Topic C: Working in the Outline tab

Explanation

PowerPoint 2002 provides you with views in which you can review your slides. You can also create new slides or an entire presentation in these views. The two main views are Normal view and Slide Sorter view. You can switch to these views by clicking the buttons in the lower-left corner of the PowerPoint window, as shown in Exhibit 2-6.

Normal view

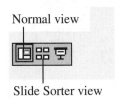

Slide Sorter view

Exhibit 2-6: The view buttons

Creating slides in the Outline tab

The Outline tab shows the slide text in outline form. It helps you to organize and develop the contents of your presentation. A slide icon and number appear to the left of each slide title. You can use the Outline tab to rearrange text within a slide and to move slides from one position to another in a presentation.

In the Outline tab, the text is arranged into five levels, each of which is indented from the left margin. The title appears at the leftmost level; bulleted items and other elements appear at subsequent levels.

To insert a new slide in the Outline tab:

1 Select the slide icon after which you want to insert the new slide.

2 Click the New Slide button on the Standard toolbar.

3 From the Slide Layout task pane, select a layout for the slide.

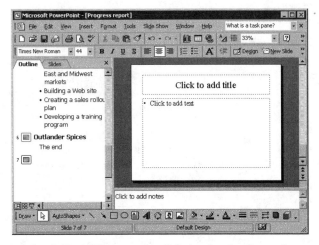

Exhibit 2-7: Adding a new slide in the Outline tab

Do it!   **C-1: Adding a bullet slide in the Outline tab**

Here's how	Here's why
1 Open Progress report	From the current unit folder.
2 Click the **Outline** tab	On the left side of the PowerPoint window.
3 Click the last slide icon	(You might need to scroll down in the Outline tab.) You'll insert a new slide at the end of the presentation.
4 Click the New Slide button	New Slide
	(On the Formatting toolbar.) A new slide is inserted in the presentation. Note that the slide layout is Title and Text.
Observe the Outline tab	The insertion point appears next to the slide icon.
5 Select the title placeholder	(On the slide.) To add a title to the slide.
Type **Performance**	
6 Select the bullet-list placeholder	To add items to the bulleted list.
7 Type **Pricing**	
Press ⏎ ENTER	To add a second bullet.
8 Type **Lower than competitors**	
Press ⏎ ENTER	To add a third bullet.
9 Add the rest of the bullet text as shown	Performance • Pricing • Lower than competitors • Products • Quality • Brand loyalty
10 Save the presentation as **My progress report**	In the current unit folder.

The Promote and Demote buttons

Explanation

After you add bullet-list items to your slide, you can move them to different levels in the list. Initially, all bullet-list items are at the same level. To move an item up or down, select it and click the *Promote* or *Demote* button on the *Outlining* toolbar. You can see the Outlining toolbar by choosing View, Toolbars, Outlining. You use the Promote button to move the selected item up one level; you use the Demote button to move the selected item down one level. If you use the Promote button on the title of a slide, the entire slide is incorporated into the previous slide as text.

Using the Promote and Demote buttons in various views

Although you might find it easier to work with bullets in the Outline tab, you can also promote and demote bullets in Normal view. To promote or demote a bullet-list item in any view:

1 Choose View, Toolbars, Outlining to display the Outlining toolbar.

2 Place the insertion point within the bulleted-list item you want to promote or demote.

3 Click Promote to move the item up one level in the list, or click Demote to move the item down one level in the list.

Do it!

C-2: Using the Promote and Demote buttons

Here's how	Here's why
1 Choose **View**, **Toolbars**, **Outlining**	(If necessary.) To view the Outlining toolbar. It appears on the left side of the window.
2 Select **Lower than competitors**	(From the slide.) You'll demote this bullet item.
3 Click ➡	(The Demote button is on the Outlining toolbar.) To demote the selected bullet item.
Observe the bullet text	You'll see that the selected bullet item is demoted by one level.
4 Select the remaining bullet items	You'll demote them as a group.
5 Click ➡	To demote the selected bullet items.
6 Select **Products**	You'll promote this bullet item.

7 Click ⬅   (The Promote button is on the Outlining toolbar.) To promote the bullet item.

Deselect and observe the slide

Performance
• Pricing
– Lower than competitors
• Products
– Quality
– Brand loyalty

You'll see bullet text at two levels.

8 Update the presentation

Topic D: Rearranging and deleting slides

Explanation

After you create a presentation, you might decide to rearrange the order in which the slides appear, or you might find that the information in some slides is no longer necessary and the slides need to be removed from the presentation.

Rearranging slides in the Outline tab

You can rearrange slides in the Outline tab by selecting a slide and dragging it to a new position. When you click the slide's icon, you'll notice that the entire text of the slide is selected. As you drag, the insertion point shows you where the slide will appear after you release the mouse button.

Do it!

D-1:   Rearranging slides in the Outline tab

Here's how	Here's why
1 Click the last slide icon	You'll move this slide.
2 Drag the slide before slide 3 as shown	2 ▦ **Outlander Spices** • Project justification • Performance • Progress-to-date • Outstanding issues 3 ▦ **Progress-to-date** • Assembled an inter team • Retained a project management consultant
Observe the pointer and the line	The shape of the pointer changes to a double-headed arrow and, when you drag the mouse, a line is displayed to mark the slide's new position.
Release the mouse button	To move the slide up in the order.
3 Observe the slides	You'll see that the slide numbers are automatically rearranged.
4 Update the presentation	

Slide Sorter view

Explanation

In Slide Sorter view, you can see all the slides in your presentation at the same time (as shown in Exhibit 2-8). This makes it easy to add, delete, and move slides. You can switch to Slide Sorter view by choosing View, Slide Sorter or by clicking the Slide Sorter View button.

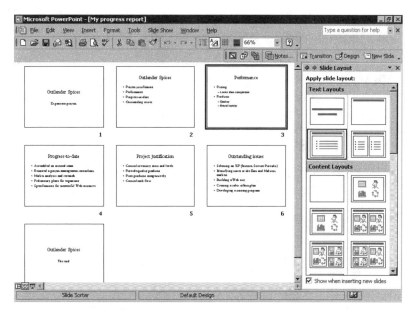

Exhibit 2-8: Slide Sorter view

Rearranging slides in Slide Sorter view

Because all slides in a presentation are visible in Slide Sorter view, it's easy to rearrange them. You can move a slide by selecting and dragging it to a new location in the presentation.

Do it!

D-2:   Rearranging slides in Slide Sorter view

Here's how	Here's why
1 Click ⊞	To switch to Slide Sorter view.
Observe the screen	You'll see miniature versions of all the slides in your presentation.
2 Observe the blue border around slide 3	You were working on this slide when you switched to Slide Sorter view. A border appears around the slide that's currently active.
3 Select the fifth slide	You'll move this slide.
Drag the slide before the third slide	
	A line indicates where it will appear.

4 Observe the slides	You'll see that the slides have been rearranged and that the slide numbers reflect the new order of the presentation.
5 Update the presentation	

Deleting slides in Slide Sorter view

Explanation

You can delete slides when you no longer need them. To delete a slide, select it and choose Edit, Delete Slide. Or, you can select the slide and press the Delete key.

Do it!

D-3: Deleting a slide in Slide Sorter view

Here's how	Here's why
1 Select the seventh slide	You'll delete this slide because it's no longer required for the presentation.
2 Press (DELETE)	To delete it.
Observe the presentation	There are only six slides now.
3 Click the Normal View button	To switch to Normal view.
4 Update the presentation	
5 Choose **View**, **Toolbars**, **Outlining**	To close the Outlining toolbar.
6 Close the presentation	Choose File, Close.

Topic E: Using slides from other presentations

Explanation

As you build a new presentation, you might want to include content that already exists in another presentation. Instead of recreating this content from scratch, you can save time and effort by inserting existing slides into your new presentation. This can be especially useful when a slide contains a complex graphic or chart.

Inserting existing slides from another presentation

When you insert a slide from one presentation into another, the inserted slides adopt the color and design of the presentation you insert them into. You can insert slides individually, or you can insert multiple slides simultaneously.

Changing the slide layouts

If you want to use a different layout for a slide, you can apply another layout style by using the task pane. To change the layout of a slide, select the slide for which you want to change the layout and from the Slide Layout task pane, select a new layout style.

Do it!

E-1: Inserting slides from another presentation

Here's how	Here's why
1 Create a new, blank presentation with a title slide	Choose File, New and in the New Presentation task pane, click Blank Presentation.
2 Click the title placeholder	
Enter **Sales update**	As the title for the slide.
3 Click the subtitle placeholder	
Enter **Corporate plans**	
4 Choose **Insert, Slides from Files...**	To open the Slide Finder dialog box.
Click **Browse**	You'll locate the presentation from which you'll insert slides.
Navigate to the current unit folder	To view a list of existing presentations in the current unit folder.
5 Select **Progress report**	
Click **Open**	To view the slides in the selected presentation.
6 Under Select slides, click slide 3	To select the Progress-to-date slide.
Click slide 5	To select the Outstanding issues slide as well.

7	Click **Insert**	To insert slides 3 and 5 into the new presentation.
	Click **Close**	To close the dialog box.
	Observe the presentation	The two slides are now part of the new presentation.
8	Save the presentation as **My sales update**	(In the current unit folder.) Choose File, Save As.
	Close the presentation	

Unit summary: Building new presentations

Topic A   In this unit, you learned how to create a new presentation by using the **File**, **New** command and the **New Presentation task pane**. You also learned how to add slides to your presentation and select different slide layouts from the **Slide Layout task pane**. Then, you used the **AutoContent Wizard** to create a presentation.

Topic B   Next, you learned how to **save a presentation** for the first time by using the **Save As dialog box**. You saved presentations in an **existing folder** and a **new folder**. You also learned how to **update** the presentation by using the **Save button**.

Topic C   Next, you learned that the **Outline tab** shows you the information in your presentation by slide and level. You learned how to create slides in this tab and how to **promote** and **demote** text to different levels.

Topic D   Then, you learned how to **rearrange** slides. You saw that this was possible in the Outline tab but easier in Slide Sorter view. Then, you learned how to **delete** slides by using the **Delete key**.

Topic E   Finally, you learned how to **insert slides** from one presentation into another presentation.

Independent practice activity

1 Create a new blank presentation.

2 Add a Title slide and add text to it.

3 Add a Bulleted List slide and enter text in it.

4 Save the presentation as **My practice presentation** in the current unit folder.

5 Add another Bulleted List slide to the presentation and enter text in it.

6 Update the presentation.

7 Switch to Slide Sorter view.

8 Move slide 3 before slide 2.

9 Update and close the presentation.

Unit 3

Formatting and proofing

Unit time: 60 minutes

Complete this unit, and you'll know how to:

A Use the Formatting toolbar, change font type and size, change bullet styles, and repeat formatting.

B Use the Cut, Copy, and Paste commands.

C Examine the on-screen rulers, set tabs, and align text.

D Check the spelling in a presentation by using the three different methods.

E Examine AutoCorrect and check the style of the presentation by using the Style Checker.

Topic A: Exploring text formatting

Explanation

How you choose to format the text in a presentation is important. Using the appropriate font type, font size, and font style can make your presentation more effective.

Using the Formatting toolbar

The *Formatting toolbar* is located below the Standard toolbar. You can select text in your presentation, then change the font type, or increase or decrease the font size. You can also apply bold, italics, or underlining to the text.

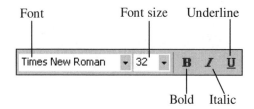

Exhibit 3-1: The Formatting toolbar

Do it!

A-1:   Using the Formatting toolbar

Here's how	Here's why
1 Open Project phase one	(From the current unit folder.) You'll be formatting the text in this presentation.
2 Click the **Slides** tab	(If necessary.) You'll work in this view.
3 Choose **View, Task Pane**	(If necessary.) To hide the task pane.
4 Double-click **Outlander**	To select the word "Outlander." You'll format the title of the first slide.
5 Click **B**	(The Bold button is on the Formatting toolbar.) To apply bold formatting to the word.
6 Apply bold formatting to the word spices	Double-click the word and click the Bold button.
7 Double-click **Project**	(In the subtitle placeholder.) You'll italicize this word.
8 Click *I*	(The Italic button is on the Formatting toolbar.) To apply italics to the word.
9 Apply italics to the words phase one	Select the words and click the Italic button.
10 Save the presentation as **My project phase one**	

Changing font type and size

Explanation

You can change the appearance of text by changing its attributes. To enhance the effectiveness of your presentation, whether you're presenting it on-screen or from overhead transparencies, it's a good idea to increase the font size and font type of titles and subtitles to make them stand out.

When you change text in Normal view, you must select the text before you can apply the attributes. You can also format text directly in the Outline tab.

Do it!

A-2: Changing the font type and size

Here's how	Here's why
1 Double-click **Outlander**	You'll make the title larger.
2 On the Formatting toolbar, click the Font Size drop-down arrow	To display a list of font sizes.
3 Select **60**	To increase the font size.
4 On the Formatting toolbar, click the Font drop-down arrow	To display a list of fonts.
Select **Courier New**	To change the font type.
5 Change the font size of spices to 60 point	Double-click the word, click the Font Size drop-down arrow, and select 60.
6 Change the font type of spices to Courier New	Click the Font drop-down arrow and select Courier New.
7 Update the presentation	

The Format Painter

Explanation

By using the Format Painter, you can quickly create consistent text formatting throughout your presentation. The Format Painter button is on the Standard toolbar. When you click the Format Painter, it copies the formatting of the previously selected text. You can then apply this formatting to other text by simply selecting it. This tool can save you time because you can apply complex formatting options in a single step.

To use the Format Painter:

1 Select the text from which you want to copy the formatting.
2 Click the Format Painter button on the Standard toolbar.
3 Select the text to which you want to apply the copied formatting.

Do it!

A-3: Using the Format Painter to repeat text formatting

Here's how	Here's why
1 Click ▣	(If necessary.) To switch to Normal view.
2 Move to the first slide	If necessary.
3 Select **Outlander spices**	The title of the first slide.
4 Click 🖌	(The Format Painter button is on the Standard toolbar.) You'll apply the formatting of the selected text to text on another slide.
5 Press (PAGE DOWN)	To move to the next slide.
6 Point to the slide	▨Ị Notice that the pointer has changed to an I-beam with a paintbrush next to it.
7 Select **Outlander spices**	On the second slide.
Observe the selected text	The formatting from the first slide's title is applied to the selected text.
8 Update the presentation	

Changing bullet styles

Explanation

When you want to emphasize certain bulleted slides or when you have a two-level bulleted list, you can change the bullet styles. To do so, choose Format, Bullets and Numbering and select one of the bullet styles shown.

Do it!

A-4: Changing bullet styles

Here's how	Here's why
1 Move to the second slide of the presentation	(If necessary.) You'll see a bulleted slide.
2 Select the text as shown	
	You'll change the bullet style.
3 Choose **Format, Bullets and Numbering...**	To display the Bullets and Numbering dialog box.
4 Observe the dialog box	By default, the previously applied bullet style is selected.
5 Select the style shown	
Click **OK**	To apply the new bullet style.
6 Observe the slide	The bullet style changes.
7 Update the presentation	

AutoNumber bullets

Explanation

By using AutoNumber bullets, you can number the items in a bulleted list automatically. When you apply AutoNumber bullets, any item you add to the list is numbered sequentially according to the previous bullet's number.

To use AutoNumber bullets:

1 Select the text to which you want to apply AutoNumber bullets.

2 Choose Format, Bullets and Numbering to open the Bullets and Numbering dialog box.

3 Click the Numbered tab.

4 Select the required numbering style.

5 Click OK.

Do it!

A-5: Using AutoNumber bullets

Here's how	Here's why
1 Move to the seventh slide	
2 Select the bulleted text	On the slide.
3 Choose **Format, Bullets and Numbering...**	To display the Bullets and Numbering dialog box.
Click the **Numbered** tab	
4 Select the indicated Number style	
Click **OK**	
5 Place the insertion point at the end of the fifth bullet	Click at the end of the word "program."
6 Press (↵ ENTER)	To create a new line.
Observe the slide	The new line is numbered accordingly.

7 Type **New employees**	The text size adjusts to fit the additional bullet text.
Press (↵ ENTER)	
8 Type **Training**	To add a seventh bullet.
9 Select the sixth numbered item	The item containing the text "New employees."
Press (DELETE)	To delete this item from the list.
Observe the list	The numbering adjusts automatically.
10 Update the presentation	

Topic B: Moving and copying text

Explanation

You can move and copy text and objects from one slide to another or from one presentation to another. This can be a significant time saver as you reorganize a presentation. It also is useful if you want to use a portion of an existing slide in another presentation.

When you move or copy text or objects, PowerPoint places the selected text or object on the *Windows Clipboard*. The Windows Clipboard is a temporary storage area that holds the text or object until you tell PowerPoint where to place it in a document. The Windows Clipboard can hold only one selection at a time and is cleared when you shut down your computer.

The Cut and Paste commands

When you want to move text or an object from one location to another, you use the *Cut* command. The Cut command removes the selected text or object from the current slide and places it on the Windows Clipboard. To place the text or object in a new location—on the same slide, on another slide, or in a different presentation altogether—you use the *Paste* command. The Paste command takes the text or object from the Windows Clipboard and inserts it wherever you position the insertion point.

To move text or an object:

1 Select the text or object that you want to move.
2 Choose Edit, Cut or click the Cut button on the Standard toolbar.
3 Place the insertion point wherever you want to insert the text or object.
4 Choose Edit, Paste or click the Paste button on the Standard toolbar.

Do it!

B-1: Moving text to another slide

Here's how	Here's why
1 Insert a new bulleted list slide at the end of the presentation	Move to the last slide, click the New Slide button, and from the task pane, select the Title and Text slide layout, if necessary.
2 Move to the second slide	
Select **Outlander spices**	The title of the slide.
3 Click ✂	(The Cut button is on the Standard toolbar.) To remove the title from the slide and place the text on the Windows Clipboard.
Move to the last slide	

4 Click in the title placeholder

Click 📋   (The Paste button is on the Standard toolbar.) To
                                      paste the text from the Windows Clipboard to
                                      the title placeholder.

Observe the slide   The title text is inserted from the Clipboard.
                                      Note that the Paste Options button appears on
                                      the slide.

5 Click as shown

                                      To display paste options.

Select **Keep Text Only**   The text formatting is lost.

Click the Paste Options button   (If necessary.) To display paste options.

Select **Keep Source   The pasted text has the same formatting as the
Formatting**   source or copied text.

6 Update the presentation

The Copy command

Explanation   When you want to copy text or an object from one location to another, you use the *Copy*
command. The Copy command creates a copy of the selected text or object on the
Windows Clipboard. This is different from the Cut command because the selected text
isn't removed from the slide. However, you use the Paste command to complete the
copy procedure.

To copy text or an object:

1 Select the text or object that you want to copy.

2 Choose Edit, Copy or click the Copy button on the Standard toolbar.

3 Place the insertion point wherever you want to insert the text or object.

4 Choose Edit, Paste or click the Paste button on the Standard toolbar.

Do it!

B-2: Copying text to another slide

Here's how	Here's why
1 Move to the second slide	
2 Select the bulleted text	Drag to select all the bullets.
3 Click 🖹	(The Copy button is on the Standard toolbar.) To copy the selected text to the Windows Clipboard.
4 Move to the last slide	
Click the bullet list placeholder	
5 Click 📋	(The Paste button is on the Standard toolbar.) To insert the copied text.
Observe the slide	The bullet items you copied from the second slide are inserted.
6 Switch to Slide Sorter view	
7 Select the second slide	
Press DELETE	To delete the second slide.
8 Switch to Normal view	
Hide the task pane	Choose View, Task Pane.
Update the presentation	

The Office Clipboard

Explanation

In addition to the standard Windows Clipboard, Office 2002 provides the *Office Clipboard*. These clipboards differ in that the Office Clipboard can store multiple items and it's integrated across all Office programs. Because of the Office Clipboard's expanded capacity, you can use it to copy several items in succession and then paste them—one at a time or simultaneously—into the desired location(s) in your presentation. This procedure is called *collect and paste*. Because this tool is integrated across Office 2002, you can use it in any Office program—Word, Excel, Outlook, Access, or PowerPoint.

In order to use the collect and paste procedure, you must use the Clipboard task pane, which you can display by choosing Edit, Office Clipboard.

Collect and paste

When you collect and paste multiple items, the items can come from any program that has the Copy command. You can paste the collected items into Word, Excel, PowerPoint, Access, or Outlook (the five core programs of Office 2002) by using the Clipboard toolbar. For example, you can copy a chart in Excel, switch to Word and copy part of a document, switch to Internet Explorer and copy some text, and then switch to PowerPoint and paste the collected items in any order.

To copy an item to the Office Clipboard, select the item and use the standard copy procedures—for example, by pressing Ctrl+C.

The Clipboard task pane

You can copy a maximum of 24 items to the Clipboard. The Office Clipboard can hold any type of data that the Windows Clipboard can hold. The last item copied to the Office Clipboard also is copied to the Windows Clipboard. Even when you close the Clipboard task pane, its contents aren't cleared.

Exhibit 3-2: The Clipboard task pane

The following table describes the buttons on the Office Clipboard:

Button	Description
Paste All	Pastes all of the collected items simultaneously at the insertion point. The items are pasted in the order they were collected.
Clear All	Clears the contents of the Office Clipboard.
Paste	Pastes the selected item at the insertion point.
Delete	Clears the selected item from the Office Clipboard.

Do it!

B-3: Discussing the Office Clipboard

Question	Answer
1 What are two differences between the Office Clipboard and the Windows Clipboard?	
2 What must you display to use the Collect and Paste feature of the Office Clipboard?	
3 Can you add items to the Office Clipboard if you aren't working in an Office application?	

Topic C: Setting tabs and alignment

Explanation

You can determine how text is positioned on your slides. Tools for aligning your text include the on-screen ruler, tabs, four text alignments menu options, and three alignment buttons.

Examining the ruler

You can use the vertical and horizontal *rulers* to adjust *indents* and tabs in the text. Indents define the left and right sides of a paragraph relative to the margins of the slide. You can set indents without changing the margins of a slide so that a block of text stands out from all the other text around it.

You can set indents easily on the ruler. The ruler contains two indent markers to help you set indents. These are the first-line or upper indent marker and the left or lower indent marker. The first-line indent marker is the down triangle on the left side of the ruler. You use it to control the left boundary for the first line of a paragraph. The lower indent marker is the box on the left side of the ruler. You use it to control the position of the second line of a paragraph, a bulleted or numbered list, and the indent of the text next to a bullet or a number.

You can also move and align objects with the ruler. As you move the mouse pointer, you can follow its movements on the ruler to show your location on the slide.

The rulers appear on the top and left sides of the slide, as shown in Exhibit 3-3. If necessary, choose View, Ruler to display the two rulers.

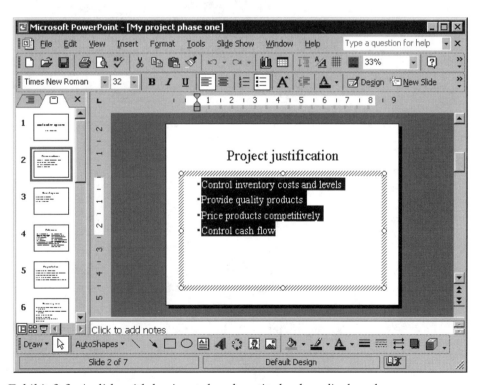

Exhibit 3-3: A slide with horizontal and vertical rulers displayed

C-1: Examining the ruler

Here's how	Here's why
1 Move to the second slide in the presentation	You'll see a bulleted slide titled "Project justification."
2 Choose **View**, **Ruler**	To display the horizontal and vertical rulers.
3 Select the bullet-list area	(As shown in Exhibit 3-3.) You'll see the indent markers on the ruler.
Observe the horizontal ruler	The upper and lower indent markers are at the ½" mark.
4 Drag the upper indent marker as shown	
	To move the upper indent marker to 1".
Observe the slide	You'll see that moving the upper indent marker moves the text, but not the bullets.
5 Drag the lower indent marker as shown	
	To move the lower indent marker to 2".
Observe the slide	The bullet text moves to 2" while the bullets remain at 1".
6 Update the presentation	

Setting tabs

The slides in your presentation don't have any lines or grids to guide you as you enter text and values. However, you can set *tabs* or *tab stops* to determine where you will enter your text and to ensure that text and values are aligned. You can set as many tabs as you want. To set and clear a tab:

1 Select the text where you want to set tab stops.

2 Click the Tab button (located to the left of the horizontal ruler) to display the type of tab that you want: left, right, center, or decimal.

3 On the ruler, click where you want to set the tab.

4 To clear a tab stop, drag the tab marker off the ruler.

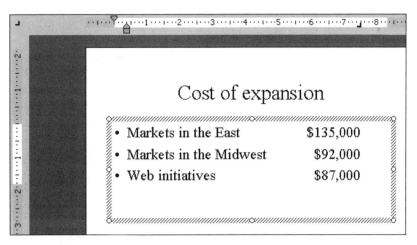

Exhibit 3-4: A part of a slide with a right tab

Do it!

C-2:   Setting tabs

Here's how	Here's why
1 Move to the third slide in the presentation	You'll see a bulleted slide titled "Cost of expansion."
2 Select the bulleted text	To display the Tab button.
Observe the Tab button	The Tab button is above the vertical ruler.
3 Click the right tab	(The right tab.) You might have to click the tab until you see the right tab.
4 Click the horizontal ruler at **7½"** as shown	To set a right tab at 7½".
5 Place the insertion point after **East**	The last word of the first bullet text.
Press ⬚TAB⬚	You'll enter a value.
6 Enter **$135,000**	
Press ⬚↓⬚	To move the insertion point to the end of the next line.
Press ⬚TAB⬚	

7	Enter **$92,000**	
	Press ⬇	To move the insertion point to the end of the next line.
	Press TAB	
8	Enter **$87,000**	
	Observe the values	You'll see that all the values are right aligned, as shown in Exhibit 3-4.
9	Update the presentation	

Changing text alignment

Explanation

Text is *left aligned* when the lines of text are aligned along the left side of the slide and the right side of the paragraph appears ragged. Text is *right aligned* when the lines of text are aligned along the right side of the slide. You can *justify* text to align it so that the lines end evenly at the left and the right sides of the slide.

To align text in your presentation, choose Format, Alignment, then choose Align Left, Align Right, Center, or Justify. You can also use the align buttons on the Formatting toolbar.

Do it!

C-3: Changing text alignment

Here's how	Here's why
1 Move to the fourth slide in the presentation	You'll see a slide titled "Performance."
Select the left-side text	You'll change the alignment of the entire left side of the slide.
2 Click ▤	(The Align Right button is on the Formatting toolbar.) To align the text to the right.
Deselect and observe the text	Performance Our pricing typically undercuts our competitors, yet still provides a large margin of profit for distributors. Our products are manufactured for quality, and have earned end-user loyalty resulting in repeat sales.	Our products move! Inventory typically turns over 50 percent faster than competitive products. Our customers have saved up to 14% of inventory cost while improving productivity and cost flow. Sales to restaurants have never been better.
	The left-side text is aligned to the right; the right-side text is still aligned to the left.

3 Select the left-side text

4 Click ▤   (The Center button is on the Formatting toolbar.) To align the left-side text to the center.

5 Select the right-side text   You'll change its alignment.

6 Change the alignment to Center   Click the Center button.

   Deselect the text

   Observe the slide

Performance

| Our pricing typically undercuts our competitors, yet still provides a large margin of profit for distributors. | Our products move! Inventory typically turns over 50 percent faster than competitive products. |
| Our products are manufactured for quality, and have earned end-user loyalty resulting in repeat sales. | Our customers have saved up to 14% of inventory cost while improving productivity and cost flow. Sales to restaurants have never been better. |

Both text boxes have center-aligned text.

7 Update the presentation

Topic D: Using the Spelling checker

Explanation

When you misspell a word, by default, it will be underlined in red. You can correct the spelling by choosing Tools, Spelling, by pressing F7, or by clicking the Spelling button on the Standard toolbar. Using any of these methods displays the Spelling dialog box. You can check the spelling in a presentation from any view.

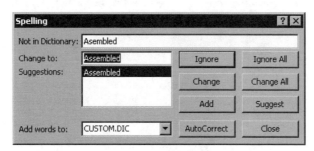

Exhibit 3-5: The Spelling dialog box

Do it!

D-1:   Checking the spelling in a presentation

Here's how	Here's why
1 Move to the first slide of the presentation	You'll check the spelling in the entire presentation.
2 Choose **Tools**, **Spelling...**	To display the Spelling dialog box.
Observe the window	You'll see the fifth slide. This is the first slide with incorrect spelling. The incorrectly spelled words are underlined in red as well as highlighted.
Observe the Spelling dialog box	You'll see options to correct the spelling, as shown in Exhibit 3-5.
3 Click **Change**	You'll see that the misspelled word "Asembled" has changed to "Assembled." Now, the text "mangement" is selected.
4 Change the spelling	Click Change to enter the correct spelling of management.
Click **Close**	To close the dialog box.
5 Press (F7)	To open the Spelling dialog box. You'll continue to check the spelling by using the shortcut key.

6	Change the spelling	To correct the spelling of preliminary. You'll see the word "Servise" misspelled in the sixth slide
7	Change the spelling	To correct the spelling of Service.
	Close the dialog box	
8	Click [ABC✓]	(On the Standard toolbar.) To use the Spelling button to open the Spelling dialog box. The word "Devloping" is misspelled in the sixth slide.
	Change the spelling	A message box appears, indicating that the spelling check is complete.
9	Click **OK**	To close the message box.
	Deselect the text	
10	Update the presentation	

Topic E: Examining AutoCorrect and the Style Checker

Explanation

You can automatically check the style and the spelling of your presentation. AutoCorrect and the Style Checker inform you of spelling errors and style inconsistencies as you type.

Using AutoCorrect

AutoCorrect automatically corrects any typing mistakes that you make, as long as the mistakes are contained in the AutoCorrect list. You can customize AutoCorrect to include words that you often type incorrectly.

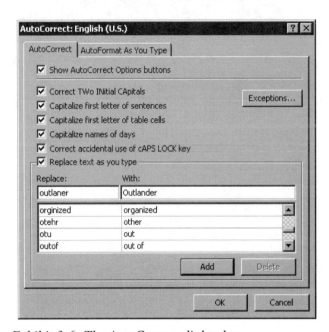

Exhibit 3-6: The AutoCorrect dialog box

Do it!   **E-1:   Using AutoCorrect**

Here's how	Here's why
1 Choose **Tools**, **AutoCorrect Options...**	To open the AutoCorrect dialog box.
Observe the dialog box	By default, all the check boxes are checked.
2 In the Replace box, enter **outlaner**	To specify the incorrect word.
3 In the With box, enter **Outlander**	To specify the correct word, as shown in Exhibit 3-6.
4 Click **Add**	To add the word to the AutoCorrect list.
5 Click **OK**	To close the AutoCorrect dialog box.
6 Place the insertion point after program	(The last word in the fifth bullet.) You'll add text here.
Press (SPACEBAR)	
7 Enter **for outlaner**	
Press (SPACEBAR)	The incorrect spelling is immediately corrected.
Enter Spices staff	To complete the bullet.
8 Update the presentation	

Using the Style Checker

Explanation
You can check your presentation for consistency of style. PowerPoint checks for style issues with punctuation, capitalization, and visual elements. PowerPoint marks style problems on a slide with a light bulb. You can ignore or correct these problems. You can also change the elements that are checked. The light bulb is only available if you turn on the Office Assistant.

Do it!

E-2:   Using the Style Checker

Here's how	Here's why
1 Move to the first slide of the presentation	You'll check the style of the presentation.
2 Choose **Tools**, **Options...**	To open the Options dialog box.
Click the **Spelling and Style** tab	You'll check the style option.
Under Style, check **Check style**	(To ensure that Style Checker works.) A message box appears asking you to enable the Office Assistant.
3 Click **Enable Assistant**	
Click **OK**	
4 Choose **Help**, **Show the Office Assistant**	To show the Office Assistant.
5 Click the title	You'll check the style of the title.
Observe the slide	
	A light bulb appears.
6 Click the light bulb	
Select **Change the text to title case**	
Observe the title	It has changed from Outlander spices to Outlander Spices.
7 Move to the next slide	You'll check the style of the rest of the slides.
Click the title	
Click the light bulb and change the text to title case	

8 Change the title text for the rest of
   the slides

   Hide the Office Assistant   (If necessary.) Choose Help, Hide the Office
                                              Assistant.

9 Choose **Tools**, **Options...**

   Activate the Spelling and Style tab   If necessary.

   Under Style, clear **Check Style**   To disable the Style Checker.

   Click **OK**

10 Update and close the presentation

Unit summary: Formatting and proofing

Topic A In this unit, you learned how to use the **Formatting toolbar** and how to apply bold and italics to text. You learned how to increase the **font size** and change the **font type**.

Topic B Then, you learned how to use the **Cut**, **Copy**, and **Paste** commands. You also learned about the **Office Clipboard**.

Topic C Then, you examined the on-screen **ruler**. You learned that you could use the ruler to adjust **indents** and **tabs** in text. Next, you learned how to **align** text. You can left align, right align, or center text.

Topic D Next, you learned how to use PowerPoint's **spelling checker**. You learned that you could choose the correct spelling from a list of suggested words.

Topic E Finally, you learned how to use **AutoCorrect** and the **Style Checker** to ensure that your presentation was error-free and consistent in style and punctuation.

Independent practice activity

1 Open Outstanding issues (from the current unit folder).

2 Make the title bold, increase the Font Size to 60, and change the Font of the title to another font type of your choice.

3 View the ruler, if necessary, and center-align the text.

4 Check the spelling in the entire presentation.

5 If necessary, choose Help, Show the Office Assistant.

6 Check the styles in the presentation.

7 Save the presentation as **My outstanding issues** and close the presentation.

8 Hide the Office Assistant, if necessary.

Unit 4

Using drawing tools

Unit time: 45 minutes

Complete this unit, and you'll know how to:

A Create objects by using the Drawing toolbar, and move and resize objects.

B Add and edit AutoShapes.

C Add text to objects, enhance the text by using the Formatting toolbar, and draw text boxes.

D Enhance objects by using fill color options.

Topic A: Drawing objects

Explanation

You can use *drawing objects*—such as rectangles, ovals, lines, and other shapes—to enhance your presentations. You can add these objects by using the *Drawing* toolbar and edit them as you would any other PowerPoint object.

The Drawing toolbar

By default, PowerPoint displays the Drawing toolbar at the bottom of the window. This toolbar has buttons you can use to draw and enhance objects. By using the Draw button, you can also group, order, flip, and rotate objects, as well as move objects in front of or behind each other. You can also apply shadow and 3-D effects to the drawn objects. Finally, you can use the Drawing toolbar to add other PowerPoint features, such as AutoShapes, WordArt, and clip art to your presentation.

To create an object by using the Drawing toolbar:

1   Click the drawing button you want to use.

2   Place the mouse pointer where you want to begin drawing. You'll see that the pointer changes to a crosshair.

3   Drag until the drawing object reaches the desired size and shape.

4   Release the mouse button. You'll see that the object is automatically selected.

Exhibit 4-1 shows a preview of the slide that you'll create in this unit.

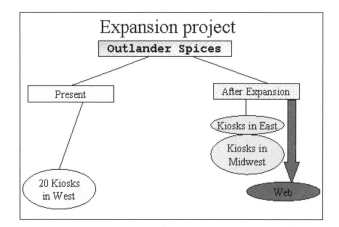

Exhibit 4-1: The completed Expansion project slide

Do it!

A-1:   Using drawing tools

Here's how	**Here's why**
1 Open Expansion project	(From the current unit folder.) This presentation contains two slides. By the end of this unit, the first slide should resemble Exhibit 4-1.
Click the **Slides** tab	(If necessary.) You'll work in this view.
2 Click ▢	The Rectangle button is on the Drawing toolbar at the bottom of the window.
Observe the pointer	The pointer changes to a crosshair when you move it inside the slide.
3 Drag to create a rectangle as shown	
Release the mouse button	
4 Select the rectangle	(If necessary.) You'll change the default fill color.
5 Choose **Format**, **AutoShape...**	To open the Format AutoShape dialog box.
Verify that the Colors and Lines tab is active	
Under Fill, from the Color list, select **No Fill**	To deselect the default fill color.
Check **Default for new objects**	To make No Fill the default for new objects.
Click **OK**	Note that the rectangle is blank.
6 Click ⬭	On the Drawing toolbar.
7 Drag to create an oval as shown, then release the mouse button	

8	Click ⬜	To draw a line.
9	Drag to create a line as shown	Expansion project
10	Save the presentation as **My expansion project**	

Duplicating objects

Explanation

After you create an object, you can duplicate it. To duplicate an object, choose Edit, Duplicate or use the shortcut key Ctrl+D.

Do it!

A-2:   Duplicating objects

Here's how	Here's why
1 Select the rectangle	You'll duplicate this rectangle.
2 Choose **Edit**, **Duplicate**	To duplicate the selected rectangle.
3 Create another duplicate of the rectangle	Select the rectangle, if necessary. Choose Edit, Duplicate.
Observe the slide	Expansion project
	The duplicates are placed on top of the original rectangle.
4 Select the oval	You'll also create a duplicate of the oval.
Press CTRL +**D**	(The shortcut key for the Duplicate command.) To duplicate the oval.
5 Create three more duplicates of the oval	You should now have five ovals.
6 Duplicate the line four times	You should now have five lines.
7 Update the presentation	

Moving objects

Explanation

You might want to move objects in a slide to reposition them. To do so:

1 Select the object. Selection handles will appear around it.
2 Point to the edge of the selected object but not to any of the selection handles. Make sure that the mouse pointer changes to a four-headed arrow.
3 Drag the object to move it to a new position.
4 Release the mouse button.

Resizing objects

You might want to resize an object after you move it. To do so:

1 Select the object. Selection handles will appear around it.
2 If you want to increase the width or height of the object, point to a horizontal or vertical selection handle. If you want to increase or decrease the size of the object while keeping the same proportions, point to a corner selection handle. In both cases, you'll see that the mouse pointer changes to a double-headed arrow.
3 Drag the selection handle until the object reaches the desired size.
4 Release the mouse button.

Do it!

A-3: Moving and resizing objects

Here's how	Here's why
1 Select the last duplicate of the rectangle	You'll move the selected rectangle.
Observe the selection handles	 The small circles around the selected object make it easy to resize the object.
2 Point to the edge of the rectangle as shown	
Observe the pointer	The mouse pointer changes to a four-headed arrow, which indicates that you can drag to move the selected object.
3 Drag to reposition the rectangle as shown	

4 Point to the selection handle as
   shown

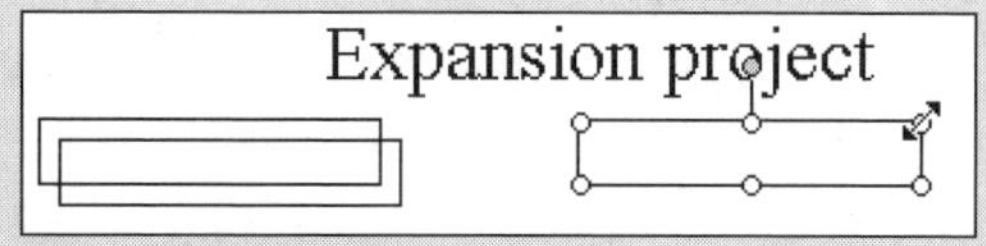

The pointer changes to a two-headed arrow.

5 Drag as shown

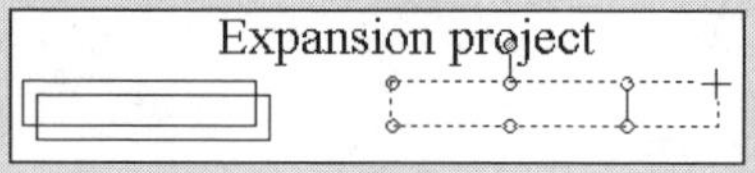

To increase the width of the rectangle.

6 Select the second duplicate of the
   rectangle

You'll move this duplicate.

   Arrange the duplicates as shown

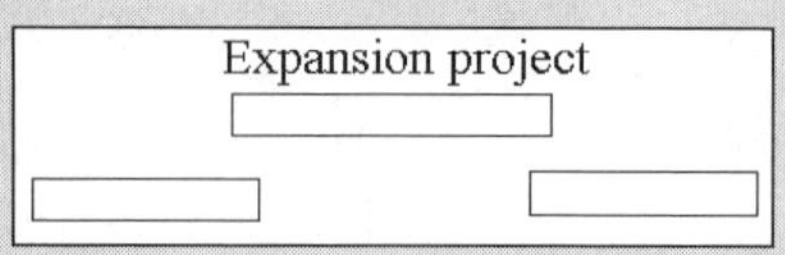

The longest rectangle should be at the top.

7 Select the last duplicate of the
   oval

You'll move the duplicate of the oval.

   Move the duplicates as shown

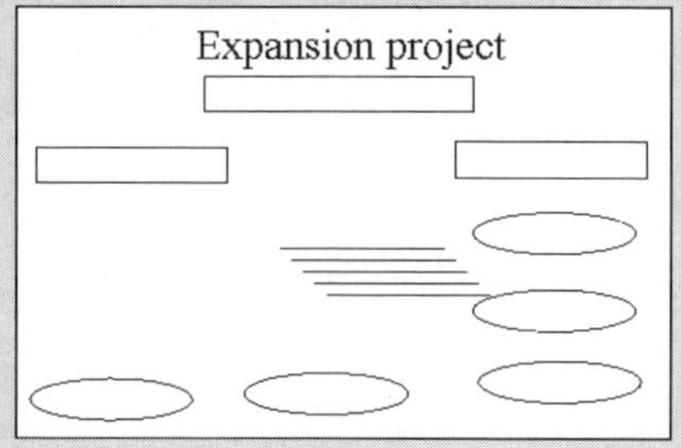

8 Select the last duplicate of the line

You'll resize and move the line.

9 Drag one end of the line to the
   oval on the left

10 Drag the other end of the line to
    the rectangle on the left

   Observe the line

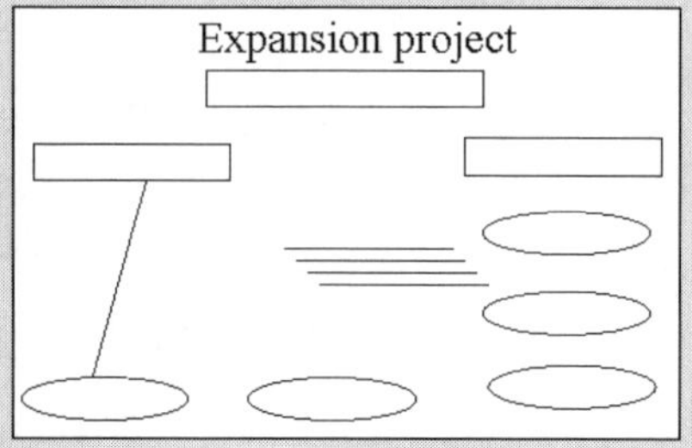

You must position the line as shown.

11 Move the other lines as shown

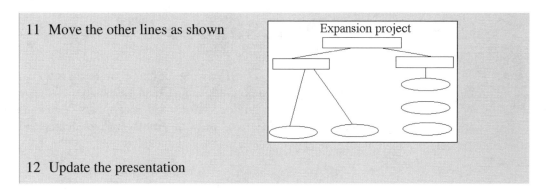

12 Update the presentation

Deleting objects

Explanation

You can delete an object that's no longer necessary by selecting the object and pressing the Delete key.

Do it!

A-4: Deleting an object

Here's how	Here's why
1 Select the line as shown	![Expansion project diagram]
2 Press ⬭DELETE⬭	To delete it.
3 Select the oval as shown	![Expansion project diagram]
4 Press ⬭DELETE⬭	To delete it.
5 Update the presentation	

Topic B: Using AutoShapes

Explanation

The *AutoShapes* menu on the Drawing toolbar contains several categories of ready-made drawing objects and includes more than 150 shapes. When you choose AutoShapes, a menu containing various options appears. You can choose a shape from one of the submenus. After you draw an AutoShape, you can edit it.

To draw an AutoShape:

1   Click AutoShapes on the Drawing toolbar.

2   Choose a menu option.

3   Choose an AutoShape from the submenu.

4   Position the mouse pointer where you want to insert the AutoShape, then drag to draw the object.

5   When the AutoShape reaches the required size, release the mouse button.

Do it!

B-1:   Using AutoShapes

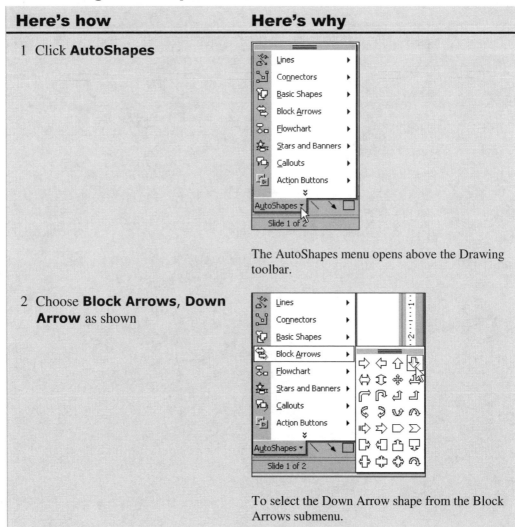

Here's how	Here's why
1 Click **AutoShapes**	The AutoShapes menu opens above the Drawing toolbar.
2 Choose **Block Arrows, Down Arrow** as shown	To select the Down Arrow shape from the Block Arrows submenu.

3 Position the mouse pointer, then drag as shown

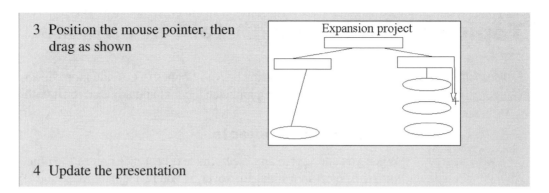

4 Update the presentation

Editing AutoShapes

Explanation

After you add an AutoShape to a slide, you can make changes to it to enhance its appearance. You can resize the object by selecting it and using its selection handles. You might even want to change the shape by adding another shape to it. To do so, you click AutoShapes and add another shape to the presentation.

Do it!

B-2: Editing AutoShapes

Here's how	Here's why
1 Select the down arrow	(If necessary.) You'll make changes to the AutoShape you just drew.
2 Select the resize handle and drag the object horizontally	To increase the width of the block arrow.
3 Select the down arrow and resize it vertically as shown	To increase the length of the down arrow.
4 Update the presentation	

Topic C: Working with text in objects

Explanation

You can add text to objects or AutoShapes to provide more information. After adding text to an object, you can enhance the text and adjust it to fit within the object.

Adding text to objects

When you add text to an object, the text becomes part of the object and moves along with the object in a slide. However, if you resize the object, the text is not resized.

Text alignment

Alignment is the positioning of text within an object. By default, the text you add to a PowerPoint object will be center-aligned.

Do it!

C-1: Adding text to an object

Here's how	Here's why
1 Select the rectangle at the top of the slide	You'll add text to it.
2 Type **Outlander Spices**	
Observe the rectangle	The text is centered within the rectangle.
3 Select the left rectangle	You'll add text to it.
4 Type **Present**	You'll add text to it.
5 Select the right rectangle	
6 Type **After Expansion**	
7 Update the presentation	

Adjusting text in objects

Explanation

By default, the text you enter in an object doesn't move onto the next line. Instead, when the text reaches the edge of the object, it flows beyond the object's boundaries. To fit text within an object, you can either resize the object or *wrap* the text to fit within the prescribed boundaries.

Text wrapping in objects

You can use the *text-wrapping* feature to adjust text within an object so that when the text reaches an object's border, it moves onto the next line rather than flowing outside the border. You can also adjust the object's size to fit the text.

To wrap text in an object:
1   Select the object.
2   Choose Format, AutoShapes.
3   In the Format AutoShape dialog box, click the Text Box tab.
4   Select Word wrap text in AutoShape.
5   Select Resize AutoShape to fit text.
6   Click OK.

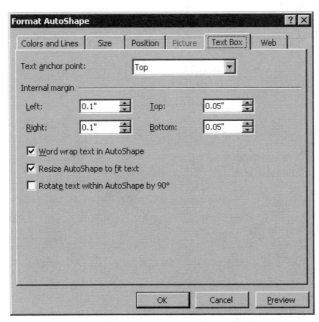

Exhibit 4-2: The Text Box tab of the Format AutoShape dialog box

Do it!

C-2:   Adjusting text in an object

Here's how	Here's why
1 Select the left oval	You'll add text to this oval.
Type **20 Kiosks in West**	
2 Observe the text in the oval	You see that the text flows outside the oval's boundaries.
3 Select the oval or the text	(If necessary.) You can select either one to enable text wrap.

4 Choose **Format**, **AutoShape...**	To open the Format AutoShape dialog box.
Click the **Text Box** tab	To display the Text Box tab.
5 Check **Word wrap text in AutoShape**	To wrap text in the object.
6 Check **Resize AutoShape to fit text**	To resize the object so that it accommodates the text.
Click **OK**	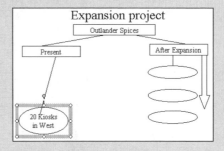

To apply the settings. You see that text wraps and the object resizes to fit it.

7 Add text to the other ovals as shown	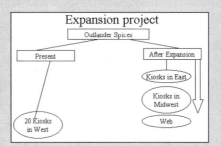
Wrap text wherever necessary	Choose Format, AutoShape, and click the Text Box tab.
8 Update the presentation	

Enhancing text in objects

Explanation

After you add text to objects, you can enhance the text to improve the look of your presentation. You can use the Formatting toolbar to enhance text. You can make the text bold, underlined, or italicized. You can also add colors to it, change its font type, or adjust its size.

Do it!

C-3:   Enhancing text in an object

Here's how	Here's why
1 Select the top rectangle	You'll enhance the text in this rectangle.
2 Click the Bold button	(On the Formatting toolbar.) To make the text bold.
3 From the Font drop-down list, select **Courier New**	To change the font style.
4 From the Font Size drop-down list, select **28**	To increase the font size.
5 Increase the width of the rectangle	If necessary.
6 Update the presentation	

Text boxes

Explanation

By default, when you select an object and type text, PowerPoint automatically creates a text box. You can also draw a text box on a slide and then enter text in the box. You can even draw a text box on a graphic object and add text. This is useful if you want to add special information to a graphic or call attention to a specific part of a chart or other graphic. By default, the text will wrap to fit in the text box.

To draw a text box and add text:

1 Click the Text Box button on the Drawing toolbar.
2 Drag to create the text box.
3 Type the text you want to add.
4 Resize and reposition the text box as necessary.

C-4: Drawing a text box in an object

Here's how	Here's why
1 Move to the second slide	
2 Click ▣	The Text Box button is on the Drawing toolbar.
3 Drag to create a text box as shown	
4 Type **Outlander Spices grows again!**	To add text to the graphic.
5 Click ▤	(The Center button is on the Formatting toolbar.) To center the text in the text box.
6 Update the presentation	

Topic D: Enhancing objects

Explanation   When you create objects, you can add fill colors to enhance them. You can also change the fill color and add a pattern or a shadow to an object.

The fill color option

By default, PowerPoint applies a fill color to all objects. You can change the default color or add a new fill color to the object by using the Fill Color button on the Drawing toolbar. You can also use this button to add a texture, pattern, or shadow to an object. You can change the style, color, and width of the line surrounding the object by using the Line Color and Line Style buttons on the Drawing toolbar.

Do it!   ### D-1:   Applying fill colors

Here's how	Here's why
1 Move to the first slide	
2 Select the top rectangle	You'll add color to the rectangle.
3 Click the Fill Color drop-down arrow	(On the Drawing toolbar.) To display the Fill Color menu.
Choose **More Fill Colors...**	To open the Colors dialog box.
4 Select any shade of blue	
Click **OK**	To apply the selected color.
Observe the Fill Color button	The button shows the last color you selected.
5 Open the Fill Color menu	
Choose **Fill Effects...**	To open the Fill Effects dialog box.
6 Under Colors, select **Two colors**	You'll add a two-color shade to the rectangle.
In the Color 2 list, verify that white is selected	To add the color white.
7 Under Shading Styles, select **Diagonal up**	You'll add this shading style to the rectangle.
Observe the Sample box	It shows a preview of the shading styles.
Click **OK**	To apply the settings.

8	Select the Present rectangle	You'll fill this rectangle.
9	Add a yellow fill to the rectangle	Choose Fill Color, More Fill Colors, then select a shade of yellow from the color palette.
	Observe the Fill Color button	The color of the Fill Color button changes to yellow.
10	Select the 20 Kiosks in West oval	
	Click [icon]	To fill the oval with the last color you selected (yellow).
11	Add a green fill color to the other objects except the arrow	
12	Update the presentation	

Moving filled objects

Explanation

When you move a filled object, you must not place the mouse pointer on any of the object's selection handles. Instead, you should place the pointer just inside the edge of the object and away from any inserted text. You'll know the pointer is in the proper position when it changes into a four-headed arrow. You can then move the object by dragging it to a new position.

Do it!

D-2: Moving a filled object

Here's how	Here's why
1 Select the Web oval	You'll reposition the object.
2 Position the mouse pointer over the selected object	
	So that the pointer changes to four-headed arrow (as shown). This indicates that you can now drag to move the object.
3 Drag as shown	
	To move the oval to the right.

4 Adjust the Kiosks in Midwest oval as shown	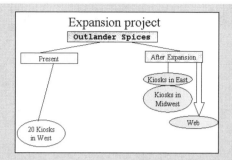
	Adjust the oval's position so that it touches the Kiosks in East oval.
5 Update the presentation	

Changing fill colors

Explanation

To make your presentation more meaningful or to increase its visual impact, you might want to change the color of some of the objects. You can do this by choosing Fill Color and applying another color from the palette.

Do it!

D-3:   Changing an object's fill colors

Here's how	Here's why
1 Select the Web oval	You'll change its color.
2 Open the Colors dialog box	From the Fill Color menu, choose More Fill Colors.
Select any shade of blue	
3 Select the down arrow	You'll add a fill color to it as well.
Apply a blue fill color to the down arrow	The Fill Color menu shows a list of all recently used colors.
4 Update the presentation	
5 Close the presentation	Choose File, Close.

Unit summary: Using drawing tools

Topic A   In this unit, you learned how to create drawing objects by using the **Drawing toolbar**. You also learned how to **resize**, **move**, and **delete** objects.

Topic B   Then, you learned how to add ready-made shapes by using the **AutoShapes** menu on the Drawing toolbar. You also learned how to edit an AutoShape.

Topic C   Next, you learned how to **add text** in objects and then enhance that text by using the Formatting toolbar. You also learned how to draw **text boxes**.

Topic D   Finally, you used the **Fill Color option** to add colors and patterns to objects. You also learned how to **move** a **filled** object and **change** the **color** of a **filled object**.

Independent practice activity

1 Create a new blank presentation with a blank slide layout.

2 Select the Horizontal Scroll AutoShape (from the Stars and Banners submenu).

3 Drag to draw the AutoShape on the slide.

4 Add Explosion 2 and 5-Point Star AutoShapes (from the Stars and Banners submenu).

5 Draw an oval by using the Drawing toolbar.

6 Add text to objects as shown in Exhibit 4-3. Wrap the text wherever necessary.

7 Make the Web Initiatives text bold. Set the font size to 32.

8 Add different fill colors to the objects.

9 Resize objects wherever required.

10 Save the presentation as **Web initiatives** in the current unit folder under the Student Data folder.

11 Close the presentation.

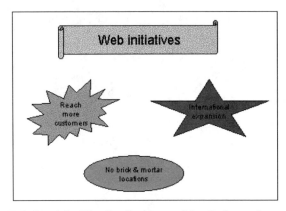

Exhibit 4-3: The final output of the Independent practice activity

Unit 5

Working with WordArt and clip art

Unit time: 45 minutes

Complete this unit, and you'll know how to:

A Use WordArt to enhance text in your presentation.

B Use the Select Picture dialog box to insert images into your slides and explore clip art on the Microsoft Web site.

Topic A: Working with WordArt

Explanation

You can use *WordArt* to add special effects to the text in your presentation. WordArt is a text object that has pre-designed effects that are applied when you create the WordArt object. Exhibit 5-1 shows a preview of the WordArt effects you'll add to a slide in this topic.

To add and edit WordArt:

1   Open the presentation.
2   On the Drawing toolbar, click Insert WordArt.
3   Select a WordArt style.
4   Click OK to open the Edit WordArt Text dialog box.
5   Enter text in the dialog box.
6   Click OK to add the WordArt to the slide.

Exhibit 5-1: A WordArt sample

Do it!

A-1: Adding and resizing WordArt

Here's how	Here's why
1 Create a new blank presentation with a blank slide layout	You'll add WordArt to a blank slide.
2 Click ▟	(The Insert WordArt button is on the Drawing toolbar.) To open the WordArt Gallery dialog box.
Observe the dialog box	It contains various styles of WordArt that you can use.
3 Select the indicated style	![WordArt] In the middle of the third row.
4 Click **OK**	To open the Edit WordArt Text dialog box.
Observe the dialog box	Here you can edit and format the WordArt text.

5	In the Font list, verify that Arial Black is selected	This will be the font type.
	In the Size list, verify that 36 is selected	This will be the font size.
6	Edit the text to read **Celebration**	
7	Click **OK**	
	Observe the slide	 The text you entered appears in the WordArt style you selected. The WordArt toolbar also appears.
8	Drag the lower-left selection handle down slightly	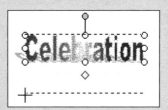 To increase the size of the WordArt.
9	Move the WordArt up as shown	 To move the WordArt to the top of the slide.
10	Save the presentation as **My celebration**	In the current unit folder.

Using the WordArt toolbar

Explanation

You can shadow, skew, stretch, align, edit, change the character spacing of, and change the shape of the text by using the various features of the WordArt toolbar, as shown in Exhibit 5-2.

Clicking the Format WordArt button opens a dialog box with six tabs. By using the Colors and Lines tab, you can change the color, fill effects, and background color of the WordArt. You can rotate the WordArt by using the Free Rotate button on the WordArt toolbar. You can click the Same Letter Heights button to make all the letters in the WordArt the same height. You can position the WordArt vertically on the slide by clicking the WordArt Vertical Text button. Finally, you can change the alignment and character spacing of your WordArt by using the Alignment and Spacing buttons at the far right end of the toolbar.

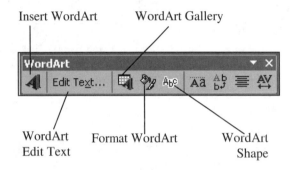

Exhibit 5-2: The WordArt toolbar

Do it!

A-2:   Using the WordArt toolbar

Here's how	Here's why
1 Select the Celebration WordArt	(If necessary.) To begin editing it.
Observe the WordArt toolbar	The toolbar, as shown in Exhibit 5-2, floats on the screen.
2 Click **Edit Text...**	(On the WordArt toolbar.) To open the Edit WordArt Text dialog box.
From the Size list, select **80**	To increase the font size.
3 Click *I*	To italicize the text.
4 Click **OK**	To increase the font size and italicize the WordArt.

5 Observe the slide

(Move the WordArt to the center of the slide, if necessary.) The text is larger and italicized.

6 Click [Abc]

(On the WordArt toolbar.) To display the WordArt Shape palette.

Observe the palette

It contains various shapes that you can use.

7 Click the indicated shape

This is the Arch Down (Curve) shape.

Observe the WordArt

The shape of the WordArt has changed.

Click anywhere on the slide

To deselect the WordArt.

8 Update the presentation

Topic B: Adding clip art

Explanation

You can add *clip art* to enhance the visual impact of your presentation. Clip art images are supplied with PowerPoint and stored in the Clip Art folder on the hard drive.

The Select Picture dialog box

The Select Picture dialog box displays a wide variety of pictures, photographs, sounds, and video clips that are ready for you to insert in your presentations. It has a search feature to help you locate the clips you need. To use the search feature, type one or more words that describe the type of clip you want in the Search text box, and then press the Enter key.

Exhibit 5-3 shows a preview of the completed slide that you'll create in this topic.

To add clip art to a slide:

1 Click the New Slide button.

2 From the Slide Layout task pane, select a layout that includes clip art. You can identify these layouts because they have a small picture of a man's head in the preview.

3 Click the clip art icon in the content placeholder.

4 From the Select Picture dialog box, select an appropriate piece of clip art.

Good News

- Party on Friday
- Two weeks vacation
- 50% of the profits to staff
- Free lunch every Wednesday
- Free parking for one month

Exhibit 5-3: A sample slide with clip art

Do it!

B-1: Inserting clip art

Here's how	Here's why
1 Click the **New Slide** button	(On the Formatting toolbar.) To add a second slide to the presentation.
2 Under Text and Content Layouts, select Title, Content and Text layout as shown	
Observe the slide	It contains placeholders for a title, content, and a bulleted list.
3 Click as shown	(You'll insert clip art in the slide.) To display the Select Picture dialog box.
Observe the dialog box	It displays several clip art images from which you can choose.
4 Select the indicated image	You need to scroll down.
Click **OK**	

5 Observe the slide	The clip art you selected appears in the clip art placeholder. The Picture toolbar appears and the WordArt toolbar closes.
6 Click the title placeholder and type **Good News**	To enter the title.
7 Click the bullet placeholder and enter five bullets as shown	• Party on Friday • Two weeks vacation • 50% of the profits to staff • Free lunch every Wednesday • Free parking for one month Press Enter after typing each bullet.
Observe the slide	The slide contains a title, clip art, and a bulleted list.
8 Update the presentation	

Working with graphics on Web

Explanation

If the graphics available in PowerPoint aren't sufficient for your needs, you can download additional graphics from the Microsoft Clip Gallery Live Web page. To access this Web page, you can use the Clips Online option from the Insert Clip Art task pane, which is available when you click the Insert Clip Art button on the Drawing toolbar or choose Insert, Picture, Clip Art.

To access the Web for graphics:

1 Click the Insert Clip Art button on the Drawing toolbar. The Insert Clip Art task pane appears.
2 In the Insert Clip Art task pane, click Clips Online.
3 Use the Microsoft Clip Gallery Live Web page to find clips.
4 Close the browser.

Do it!

B-2:   Exploring clip art on the Web

Here's how	Here's why
1 Click 🖼	(On the Drawing toolbar.) The Add Clips to Organizer message box appears.
Check **Don't show this message again**	To ensure that the message box doesn't appear again.
Click **Later**	You don't want to add clips to the Organizer.
Observe the screen	The Insert Clip Art task pane appears.
2 Click **Clips Online**	
Observe the browser window	The browser window appears with the Microsoft Design Gallery Live Home page.
3 Explore the Microsoft Design Gallery Live	You can view or search for clip art by type, keyword, or category.
4 Close the browser	
5 Close the presentation	It's not necessary to save any changes.

Unit summary: Working with WordArt and clip art

Topic A

In this unit, you learned how to **insert WordArt** into a slide. You learned to **resize**, **move**, and **change** the shape of WordArt by using the various options on the WordArt toolbar.

Topic B

Finally, you learned how to **insert clip art** into a slide by using the **Select Picture dialog box**. You also explored clip art on the Web by selecting the **Clips Online** option.

Independent practice activity

1 Create a new presentation starting with a blank slide.

2 Select a WordArt style of your choice.

3 Enter **Keys to our success**.

4 Resize the WordArt.

5 Move the WordArt to the center of the slide.

6 Insert a new slide.

7 Select the Title, Content and Text layout.

8 Enter the title **Keys to our success**.

9 Insert clip art as shown in Exhibit 5-4.

10 In the bulleted list, enter five bullets, as shown in Exhibit 5-4.

11 Compare your work to Exhibit 5-4.

12 Save the presentation as **My success** in the current unit folder, then close the presentation.

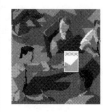

Keys to our success

- Teamwork
- Dedication
- Innovation
- Commitment
- Loyalty

Exhibit 5-4: The slide after step 10 of the Independent practice activity

Unit 6

Using tables and charts

Unit time: 45 minutes

Complete this unit, and you'll know how to:

A Add a table to a presentation and enter text in the table.

B Create and modify a chart by using Microsoft Graph.

C Create and modify an organization chart.

Topic A: Working with tables

Explanation
You can create tables in a presentation to display information in a row and column format. PowerPoint provides a layout for adding a table to your presentation.

Adding tables

Tables consist of rows and columns. The intersection of a row and a column is referred to as a *cell*. You can add text or number values to a cell. Exhibit 6-1 shows the structure of a table.

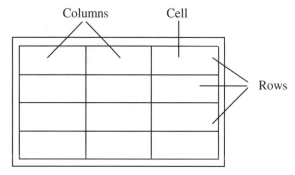

Exhibit 6-1: A sample table structure

You can add a table to a presentation by choosing Insert, Table or by inserting a new slide with the Title and Table layout. In both cases, the default table layout is two rows by two columns, which you can modify to suit your requirements. A third way to add a table is by clicking the Insert Table button on the Standard toolbar. In this way, you can specify a table with up to four rows and up to five columns. Again, you can modify this layout to suit your requirements after inserting the table.

After you insert a table, the *Tables and Borders* toolbar appears. You use this toolbar to add cells of different heights to the table and to vary the number of columns per row. You can also use it to add border styles, change the border widths, and add fill colors to the table.

Adding text to tables

You add text to a table the same way you add text to any other object. Text or number values are entered in a table's cell. You move from one cell to another by pressing the Tab key or by using the arrow keys.

Do it!

A-1: Adding a table

Here's how	Here's why
1 Open Performance	(From the current unit folder.) You'll insert a table into this presentation.
2 Click the **New Slide** button	(On the Formatting toolbar.) To insert a new slide.
3 From the Slide Layout task pane, under Other Layouts, select the Title and Table layout as shown	
4 Click the title placeholder	You'll add a title to the slide.
Type **Performance**	This will be the slide's title.
5 In the table placeholder, double-click the table icon	
Observe the Insert Table dialog box	You can specify the number of columns and rows in the table. Note that in the Number of columns box, 2 is selected. Your table will have two columns.
6 In the Number of rows box, enter **4**	
Click **OK**	To insert a table that contains two columns and four rows. The Tables and Borders toolbar appears.
Observe the Tables and Borders toolbar	This toolbar has buttons you can use to create rows and columns and enhance the table.

7	Click in the first cell of the table	(If necessary.) You'll enter text in this cell.
	Type **Price**	
8	Press (TAB)	You'll move to the next cell in the table.
	Observe the insertion point	It moves to the next cell, indicating that you can enter text here.
9	Type **Lower than competitors**	
	Press (TAB)	You'll move to the first cell in the next row.
10	Type **Inventory turnover**	
11	Complete the table as shown	

Performance

Price	Lower than competitors
Inventory turnover	50% faster than competitors
Cost	14% of inventory cost saved
Profit	132% growth in profits

	Save the presentation as **My performance**

Topic B: Creating and enhancing charts

Explanation

Charts are the graphical representations of numeric data. PowerPoint comes with a program called *Microsoft Graph*, which offers fourteen *chart* types and several formatting options for creating charts.

Using Microsoft Graph to create charts

You can create a chart by adding a slide with chart layouts. You can also choose Insert, Chart or click the Insert Chart button to add a chart. Using these methods opens the Microsoft Graph and displays two windows: the *Datasheet window* and the *Chart window*. The Datasheet window contains sample data that comes with Microsoft Graph. The Chart window displays the data in graphical form. When you insert a chart into a slide, you'll see that the menu bar displays additional menu options so you can work with the datasheet and chart.

The Datasheet window

The Datasheet window provides the data for creating a chart. The datasheet contains the legend and series labels for the chart, as well as the row and column headings, which are the dark boxes located to the left of the rows and above the columns. The cells of the datasheet contain values that form the basis for the chart. You change the data in the datasheet to meet your needs. You can also edit the row headings to change the legend and the column headings to change the series label. Finally, you can change the values in the cells to provide the information you want. To do so, point to the desired cell and enter the data. The text in the cell is replaced by the data you enter.

The Chart window

As you make changes or add data to the datasheet, the chart is automatically updated.

Do it!

B-1: Using Microsoft Graph

Here's how	Here's why
1 Click the **New Slide** button	On the Formatting toolbar.
2 From the Slide Layout task pane, select the Title and Chart layout	 You'll add a chart to your presentation.
Observe the menu bar	File Edit View Insert Format Tools Slide Show Window Help It shows the typical menu options for PowerPoint.

3 In the title placeholder, type **Comparison Chart**	This will be the slide's title.
4 Double-click the chart icon	To open the Chart and Datasheet windows.
Observe the screen	By default, PowerPoint provides sample data and a corresponding chart.
Observe the menu bar	File Edit View Insert Format Tools Data Chart Window Help
	The menu bar shows additional options to help you work with charts and datasheets.
Observe the pointer	It changes to a plus sign when you move it over the datasheet.
5 In the Datasheet, click **A**	The entire column is selected.
Click **1**	The entire row is selected.
Click **East**	To select the cell.
6 Replace East with **Outlander Spices**	To change the row heading. The new text flows over into the next cell.
Replace West with **Competitors**	
7 Click **3**	You'll delete this row.
Observe the datasheet	

1	Outlander	20.4	27.4	90
2	Competito	30.6	38.6	34.6
3	North	45.9	46.9	45
4				

	The entire row is selected.
Press (DELETE)	To delete the row.
8 Replace the column headings as shown	

A	B	C	D
Price	Inventory turnover	Cost	Profit

9 Select cell A1	You'll enter text in this cell under the Price column heading.
Enter **25**	
10 Press (↓)	To move to cell A2.
Enter **30**	

11	Select cell B1	You'll enter text under Inventory turnover.
	Enter **60**	

12 Replace the remaining values as shown

	A	B	C	D
	Price	Inventory	Cost	Profit
Outlander	25	60	35	70
Competito	30	40	50	30

13 Observe the chart — The default chart automatically updates to display the data in graphical form.

Update the presentation

Formatting charts

Explanation

You can format your chart so that its graphical representation of the data is clearer to your audience. In Microsoft Graph, you can format each individual item in the chart, or you can format the entire Chart Area. The *Chart Area* consists of four items: the plot area, the legend, the value axis, and the category axis (as shown in Exhibit 6-2). The *plot area* contains the chart along with the two axes. In Exhibit 6-2, you can see that the plot area is marked as the inner rectangle.

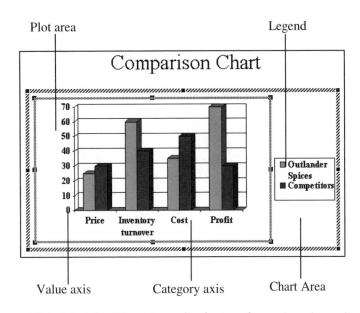

Exhibit 6-2: The Chart Area displaying the various items in a chart

Using the Format menu

When you select a chart item, the selected item becomes the first command in the Format menu. For example, when you select the plot area, the first command in the Format menu becomes Selected Plot Area. This means that you can format any item by selecting it and choosing the first command from the Format menu. You can also change the color and add borders and a shadow to the area.

Using the Chart menu

Another way to format the chart is by choosing Chart, Chart Options. The Chart Options dialog box contains tabs that offer related formatting options.

Do it!

B-2: Formatting a chart

Here's how	Here's why
1 Close the Datasheet window	Click the Close button in the upper-right corner of the Datasheet window.
2 Select the chart placeholder	If necessary.
Observe the menu bar	You'll see that the Chart menu is now available.
3 Click the plot area as shown	
4 Choose **Chart, Chart Options...**	To open the Chart Options dialog box.
5 Click the **Gridlines** tab	
6 Under Value (Z) axis, clear **Major gridlines**	You'll clear the gridlines from the plot area.
Click **OK**	To clear the gridlines.
7 Click any blue bar	
	To select the Competitors "series."

8 Choose **Format**, **Selected Data Series...**

To display the Format Data Series dialog box.

Observe the dialog box

You'll format the series by changing its color.

9 Under Area, select a yellow color

You'll change the column color to yellow.

Click **OK**

To apply the color.

10 Change the color of the Outlander Spices series to blue

Deselect the series

Click anywhere outside the plot area.

Observe the chart

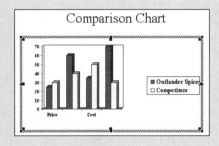

11 Choose **Chart**, **Chart Type...**

To display the Chart Type dialog box.

Observe the chart types

12 From the Chart type list, select as shown

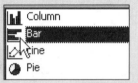

To change the chart type from Column to Bar.

Click **OK**

13 Observe the chart

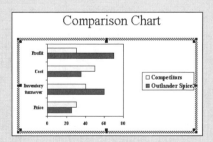

You'll see that the chart changes to a bar chart.

Deselect the chart

14 Update the presentation

Topic C: Creating organization charts

Explanation

You can display the hierarchical details of your company by using organization charts. You can add different levels to the chart and enhance it by highlighting the key levels.

Adding organization charts

To add an organization chart to a presentation, add a slide with the Title and Diagram or Organizational Chart layout from the Slide Layout task pane. You'll see a placeholder for the diagram or organization chart. Double-clicking the organization chart icon displays the Diagram Gallery dialog box, as shown in Exhibit 6-3. The Organization Chart toolbar also appears. It displays a chart template containing several boxes. By default, the template shows two levels of boxes. The topmost box is at level 1 and the boxes directly below it are at level 2. You enter text into a box by selecting the box and typing the text.

The Diagram Gallery dialog box

Using the Diagram Gallery dialog box, you can create the following types of diagrams:

- Organization Chart to show hierarchical details of your organization
- Cycle diagram to show a process that has a continuous cycle
- Radial Diagram to show the relationship of different elements in a process to a core element
- Pyramid Diagram to show foundation-based relationships in a process
- Venn Diagram to show areas of overlap between elements in a process
- Target Diagram to show steps towards a goal

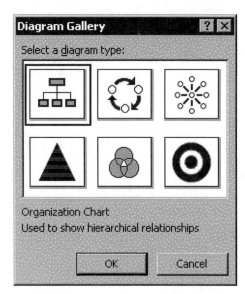

Exhibit 6-3: The Diagram Gallery dialog box

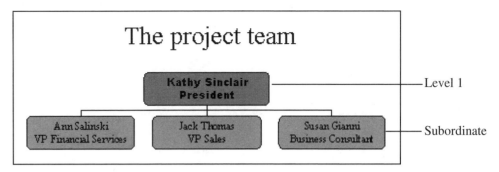

Exhibit 6-4: A sample organization chart

Do it!

C-1: Adding an organization chart

Here's how	Here's why
1 Insert a new slide	
2 In the Slide Layout task pane, under Other Layouts, select as shown	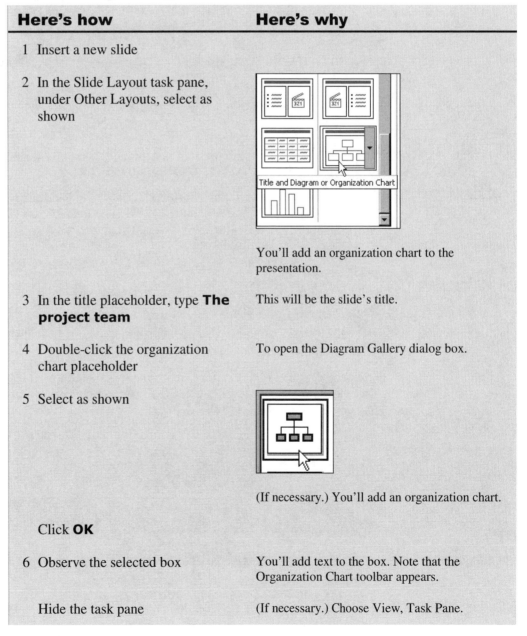 You'll add an organization chart to the presentation.
3 In the title placeholder, type **The project team**	This will be the slide's title.
4 Double-click the organization chart placeholder	To open the Diagram Gallery dialog box.
5 Select as shown	(If necessary.) You'll add an organization chart.
Click **OK**	
6 Observe the selected box	You'll add text to the box. Note that the Organization Chart toolbar appears.
Hide the task pane	(If necessary.) Choose View, Task Pane.

7	Type **Kathy Sinclair**	The name of the project leader.
	Press [↵ ENTER]	
8	Type **President**	The project leader's title.
	Deselect the box	
9	Select the first box at level 2	You'll add text to it.
	Add text as shown	
10	Add text to the remaining boxes at level 2 as shown	
	Deselect the organization chart	
11	Update the presentation	

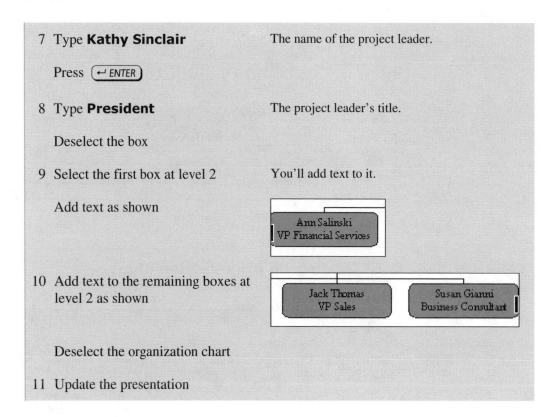

Adding levels to organization charts

Explanation

By default, an organization chart has two levels. To add additional levels to an organization chart, you must add more boxes. The Organization Chart toolbar has buttons for adding boxes at different levels. Box levels include Subordinate, Coworker, and Assistant.

To add a box:

1 Select the box to which you want to attach a new box.
2 Click the Insert Shape button on the Organization Chart toolbar to display a menu.
3 From the menu, select an appropriate option.

For example, if you want to add a Subordinate box to the second box at level 2, you select the second box at level 2. Click the Insert Shape button and select Subordinate. This creates the third level of the chart, as shown in Exhibit 6-5.

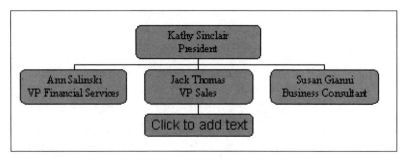

Exhibit 6-5: The organization chart showing a third level

Do it!

C-2: Adding levels to an organization chart

Here's how	Here's why
1 Select as shown	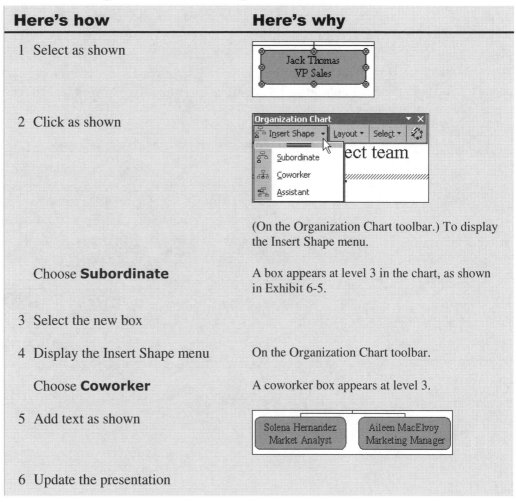
2 Click as shown	
	(On the Organization Chart toolbar.) To display the Insert Shape menu.
Choose **Subordinate**	A box appears at level 3 in the chart, as shown in Exhibit 6-5.
3 Select the new box	
4 Display the Insert Shape menu	On the Organization Chart toolbar.
Choose **Coworker**	A coworker box appears at level 3.
5 Add text as shown	
6 Update the presentation	

Formatting organization charts

Explanation

You can enhance boxes in an organization chart by adding borders, colors, and shadows to them. You can do this by using the Drawing toolbar. You can enhance the text in the boxes by using the Formatting toolbar to change its font, color, and alignment.

You can select multiple boxes and apply the same formatting to all of them. To do so, hold down the Shift key while clicking the boxes you want to select, then select the desired formatting options.

Do it!

C-3: Formatting an organization chart

Here's how	Here's why
1 Select the level 1 box	You'll change the color of the box.
2 Click as shown	
	On the Drawing toolbar.
Select a light blue color	To apply a blue color to the box.
3 From the Font list, select **Arial Black**	On the Formatting toolbar.
4 Update and close the presentation	

Unit summary: Using tables and charts

Topic A   In this unit, you learned how to **add a table** to your presentation by using the **Title and Table** layout. You also learned how to **add text** to the **table**.

Topic B   Then, you learned how to add a **Microsoft Graph** by using the **Title and Chart** layout, and you enhanced the chart by using the **Chart Options** dialog box. You also learned how to change the chart type by using the **Chart Type** dialog box.

Topic C   Finally, you learned how to **add an organization chart** to a presentation by using the **Title and Diagram or Organization Chart** layout. You also learned how to format an organization chart by changing the **color** and **font** of its boxes.

Independent practice activity

1 Create a new blank presentation with a Title and Table layout slide.

2 Type **Sales (in Pounds)** in the title placeholder.

3 Add a 5-column by 4-row table to the slide.

4 Complete the table, as shown in Exhibit 6-6.

5 Add another slide containing a title and a chart.

6 Replace the row headings with the text in the first column in the table.

7 Replace all values in the datasheet with the values in the table cells.

8 Add another slide containing an organization chart.

9 Create levels and add text, as shown in Exhibit 6-7.

10 Change the color of all boxes to yellow.

11 Compare your chart to Exhibit 6-7.

12 Run the presentation.

13 Save the presentation as **My sales** and close it.

Sales (in Pounds)

	1st Qtr	2nd Qtr	3rd Qtr	4th Qtr
Cumin	30	45	45	30
Thyme	50	80	80	60
Oregano	85	60	60	75

Exhibit 6-6: The Sales table

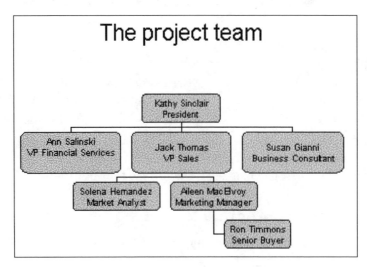

Exhibit 6-7: The completed organization chart

Unit 7

Enhancing presentations

Unit time: 45 minutes

Complete this unit, and you'll know how to:

A Create a new presentation by using a design template, apply a design template to an existing presentation, and use multiple design templates in a single presentation.

B View a slide master and edit it by changing text and bullet options.

C Insert a new slide master, use multiple slide masters, and delete a slide master from a presentation.

D Finetune the pace of your presentation by adding transition effects and timings.

E Add speaker notes, footers, and the company name to each slide.

Topic A: Using templates

Explanation

You can change the appearance of a presentation by applying a *template* to it. Templates contain color schemes, slide masters, and title masters that provide a consistent format and look to a presentation. After you apply a template, each slide you add to the presentation will have the same customized look. PowerPoint comes with a wide variety of professionally designed templates.

You can either create a new presentation based on a template or apply a different design template to an existing presentation.

To create a new presentation based on a template:

1 Choose File, New to display the New Presentation task pane.

2 In the task pane, under New, click From Design Template. The Slide Design task pane appears with various design template options.

3 Select an appropriate design template.

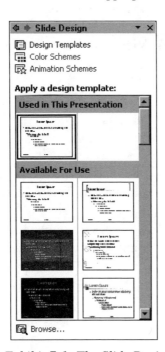

Exhibit 7-1: The Slide Design task pane

Do it!

A-1: Creating a presentation based on a template

Here's how	Here's why
1 Choose **File**, **New...**	
2 Under New, click **From Design Template** as shown	

(In the New Presentation task pane.) You'll create a new presentation from a design template.

Observe the Slide Design task pane	It displays various design templates that you can use for your presentation.
3 Under Available For Use, select **Digital Dots**	

Scroll down, if necessary.

Observe the slide	

The slide has the selected template applied to it. Note that the slide has the Title Slide layout.

4 Enter **Outlander Spices** as the title of the slide	In the title placeholder on the slide.
5 Insert a new slide	Note that the new slide has the same design template applied to it.
6 Save the presentation as **My presentation**	In the current unit folder.
Close the presentation	

Applying a design template to an existing presentation

Explanation

You apply a template to give a professional look and feel to your presentation. You can select a template depending on the purpose and audience of the presentation. When you apply a design template to an existing presentation, PowerPoint automatically updates the text styles and graphics; it also changes the color scheme of your entire presentation. To apply a design template to an existing presentation, select a slide and click the Design button on the Formatting toolbar to display the Slide Design task pane. Select an appropriate design template from the task pane.

Do it!

A-2: Changing the design template

Here's how	Here's why
1 Open Investors	From the current unit folder.
Move through the presentation	To view the slides.
2 Click **Design**	
	(On the Formatting toolbar, if necessary). Note that the Slide Design task pane displays various template designs that you can apply to your presentation.
3 Under Available For Use, select **Blends** as shown	
4 Move through the presentation	You'll see that the entire presentation has been updated with the design template that you selected.
5 Save the presentation as **My investors**	

Multiple design templates in a single presentation

Explanation

You can have multiple design templates applied in a single presentation. For example, you can have one design template for the title slide and another for the other slides in a presentation.

To apply multiple design templates in a single presentation:

1 Select the slides to which you want to apply a different design template.
2 Click the Design button on the Formatting toolbar. The task pane displays the available design templates.
3 Click the down arrow next to the design template that you want to apply to the selected slides. A pop-up menu appears.
4 Choose Apply to Selected Slides.

Do it!

A-3: Using multiple design templates in a presentation

Here's how	Here's why
1 Switch to Slide Sorter view	You'll format the title slide differently. Note that all the slides have the same design.
2 Select the first slide	(If necessary.) You'll apply a different design template to the first slide.
3 Under Available For Use, click the down arrow as shown	A pop-up menu appears.
4 Choose **Apply to Selected Slides**	To apply the design template to only the title slide.
Move through the presentation	The title slide has a design that's different from other slides.
Observe the Slide Design task pane	Note that under Used in This Presentation, two design templates appear.
5 Update and close the presentation	

Topic B: Working with the slide master

Explanation

All PowerPoint presentations have a *slide master* that controls text characteristics, background color, and certain special effects, such as shadowing and bullet styles. If you change the formatting in the slide master, the formatting for the entire presentation will be affected.

Elements of a slide master

The *Master Title Area* of the slide master controls the font, size, color, style, and alignment of the text in the title object area.

The *Master Object Area* controls the font, size, color, style, and alignment of the slide text.

You can add background items to the slide master, such as the date and/or time, slide numbers, stamps, company logos, and borders. These items will appear on every slide to which the master is applied.

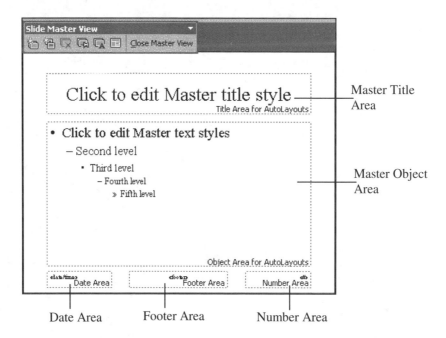

Exhibit 7-2: A slide master

Do it!

B-1:   Examining the elements of a slide master

Here's how	Here's why
1 Open Project report	From the current unit folder.
Move to the first slide	If necessary.
2 Choose **View**, **Master**, **Slide Master**	To display the slide master, as shown in Exhibit 7-2. This view is also called Master view. Note that the Slide Master View toolbar also appears.
3 Observe the Master Title Area	The Master Title Area controls the formatting of the title placeholder on the slide.
4 Observe the Master Object Area	The Master Object Area controls the formatting of the text object area on the slide.
5 Observe the Date Area	The Date Area controls the formatting of the date and time.
6 Observe the Footer Area	The Footer Area controls the formatting of the footer.
7 Observe the Number Area	The Number Area controls the formatting of the slide numbers.

Changing the font type and size on a slide master

Explanation

The slide master controls how the slides in a presentation are formatted. It contains placeholders for title, text, and background items. While creating a presentation, you can emphasize the title or some of the bullet text by changing the font size, type, or color in the slide master.

To change the slides' format in a presentation:

1   Open the slide master and select the Master Title Area.
2   Change the font type, size, or color as required.
3   Select the Master Object Area.
4   Change the font type, size, or color as required.
5   Switch to Normal view.
6   Update the presentation.

Do it!

B-2: Changing the default font

Here's how	Here's why
1 Select the **Master Title Area**	
2 From the Font list, select **Arial**	To change the title font.
Observe the Master Title Area	The font has changed.
3 From the Font Size list, select **40**	To change the title font size.
Observe the Master Title Area	The font size has changed.
4 Select the **Master Object Area**	
5 From the Font list, select **Courier New**	To change the text font.
6 From the Font Size list, select **24**	The font size for the Master Object Area has changed.
7 Click **Close Master View**	(On the Slide Master View toolbar.) To close the slide master.
8 Click the Normal View button	(If necessary.) To switch to Normal view.
Move through the presentation	You'll see that the font type and size have changed for the entire presentation.
9 Save the presentation as **My project report**	

Modifying bullets on a slide master

Explanation

The Master Object Area controls the font, size, color, style, and alignment of the slide text. You can modify the text formatting, the default bullets, and the line spacing. You can also change the bullet shape for each indent level.

To modify the default bullets:

1 Click the Master Object Area and choose Format, Bullets and Numbering.
2 Select the desired bullet style.
3 Change the bullets for each level you want to modify.
4 Click OK.

Do it!

B-3:   Modifying the default bullets

Here's how	Here's why
1 Move to the first slide	If necessary.
2 Choose **View**, **Master**, **Slide Master**	You'll modify the bullets.
3 In the Master Object Area, select the first line of text	You'll format the text.
4 Choose **Format**, **Bullets and Numbering...**	To display the Bullets and Numbering dialog box.
5 Verify that the Bulleted tab is selected	
6 Select the indicated option	

Click **OK**	To return to the slide master.
Deselect and observe the Master Object Area	

The bullet style for the first level has changed.

7 Select the second line of text

8	Open the Bullets and Numbering dialog box	Choose Format, Bullets and Numbering.
	Select the indicated option	
	Click **OK**	To return to the slide master.
9	Click **Close Master View**	(On the Slide Master View toolbar.) To switch to Normal view.
	Observe the third slide	You'll see that the bullets for both the first and second level have changed.
10	Update the presentation	

Topic C: Working with multiple slide masters

Explanation

You can have multiple slide masters in a presentation. This is very helpful if you need to use the same presentation content for different audiences. You can use one slide master to present on-screen and another slide master to provide the presentation as a hard copy. You can delete a slide master from a presentation when you no longer need it.

Inserting slide masters

You can have as many slide masters as you want in a presentation. To add a new slide master:

1   Choose View, Master, Slide Master to switch to Master view.
2   Click the Insert New Slide Master button on the Slide Master View toolbar.
3   Format the slide master to meet your needs.
4   Click the Close Master View button on the Slide Master View toolbar to close Master view.

A new slide master and a title master also get added when you apply a new design template to a presentation. This pair of slide master and title master is referred to as *slide-title master pair* and appears together in Master view. The title master controls the formatting of the title slides or the slides with Title Slide layout in a presentation.

Preserving slide masters

PowerPoint automatically deletes a slide master when it is not used by any of the slides. To prevent this, you need to *preserve* a slide master. By default, a new slide master is preserved when you insert it by using the Insert New Slide Master button on the Slide Master View toolbar.

Do it!

C-1: Inserting a new slide master

Here's how	Here's why
1 Choose **View**, **Master**, **Slide Master**	To switch to Master view.
2 In the left pane, point as shown	
	This is the default slide master that's used by all the slides in the presentation.
3 Click 	(The Insert New Slide Master button is on the Slide Master View toolbar.) To insert a new slide master.
Observe the left pane	It shows two slide masters.
4 Point to the second slide master	This is the custom design slide master that is not used by any slide.
Point as shown	
	This thumbtack icon indicates that the slide master is preserved. Also note that the first slide master is not preserved as no icon appears next to it.
5 In the Footer Area, select **<footer>**	You'll enter footer text here.
Enter **Outlander Spices**	
6 Under Available For Use, click as shown	
	A pop-up menu appears.
Choose **Add Design**	You'll add this design template to the presentation. Note that this adds two masters in the presentation.

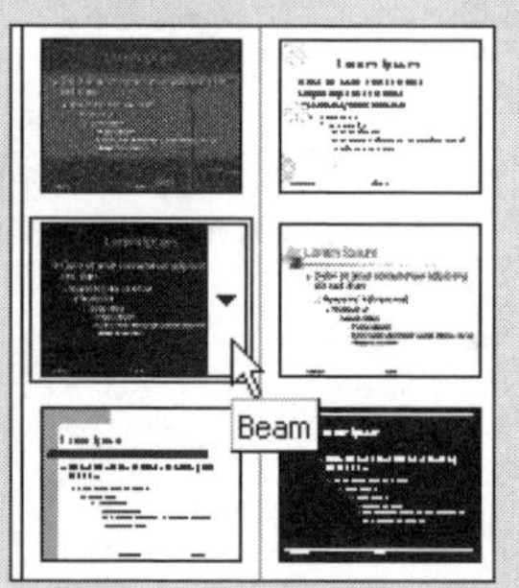

7 Observe the left pane

There are four masters now. Note the link between the last two masters. This link indicates that these two form the slide-title master pair. Note that both of these masters have the same design template.

Point to the third master

This is the Beam slide master that is not used by any slide.

Point to the fourth master

This is the Beam title master that is not used by any slide.

8 In the left pane, select the first master

You'll preserve this master.

Right-click the master

A shortcut menu appears.

Choose **Preserve Master**

(To preserve the master.) Note the thumbtack icon that appears next to the first master. This icon indicates that the master is preserved now.

9 Click **Close Master View**

Update the presentation

Applying multiple slide masters

Explanation

The Slide Design task pane displays all the slide masters for a presentation under Used in This Presentation. You can apply a different slide master to all the slides or specific slides in your presentation.

To apply a slide master to all the slides, display the Slide Design task pane, and select the slide master that you want to apply. To apply a slide master to specific slides, you need to select the slides before applying the slide master.

Do it!

C-2: Using multiple slide masters

Here's how	Here's why
1 Observe the task pane	**Apply a design template:** **Used in This Presentation**
	The presentation has three design templates since there are now three slide masters for the presentation. The first design template is selected because it applies to the entire presentation.
2 Point to the first design template	This is the default design template used by all the slides in the presentation.
3 Under Used in This Presentation, select the custom design slide master	Note that all the slides are updated with this new design template.
4 Under Used in This Presentation, select the Beam design template	Note that all the slides are updated with this new design template.
5 Update the presentation	

Deleting slide masters

Explanation

You can delete slide masters that are no longer required. When you delete a slide master that's a part of the slide-title master pair, the title master also gets deleted automatically.

You can delete a slide master in either of the following ways:

- In the Master view, select the slide master that you want to delete and click the Delete Master button on the Slide Master View toolbar.
- In the Master view, select the slide master that you want to delete and right-click to display the shortcut menu and choose Delete Master.
- In the Master view, select the slide master that you want to delete and press the Delete key.

Do it!

C-3: Deleting a slide master

Here's how	Here's why
1 Switch to Master view	Choose View, Master, Slide Master.
Observe the left pane	It shows four masters.
Point to each master and view the description	
2 Select the first master	
	You'll delete this master.
3 Click	(The Delete Master button is on the Slide Master View toolbar.) To delete the selected master.
Observe the left pane	Only three masters are left.
Close the Master view	Click the Close Master View button.
4 Update the presentation	

Topic D: Adding transitions and timings

Explanation

You can set a different transition effect for each slide in your presentation. *Transitions* are special effects that introduce a slide in a slide show. You can choose from a variety of transitions and vary their speed. You can use transition effects to indicate a new section of a presentation or to emphasize a certain slide.

To enhance the impact of graphic images or text, you can add sound effects to a presentation. PowerPoint provides several sound effects for you to use.

You can also set timings for your presentation so that you can run the slide show without using your mouse or keyboard to display the next slide. Instead, the slides will be displayed automatically at specified time intervals.

Setting transition effects

When you set transition effects for a slide from within Slide Sorter view, you can preview the transition by clicking the Transition icon below the slide. You can also preview the transition by clicking the transition icon below the slide number in the Slides tab.

To set a transition effect:

1 Select a slide.
2 Choose Slide Show, Slide Transition to display the Slide Transition task pane.
3 Select an appropriate transition option.

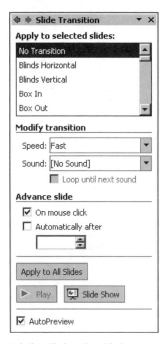

Exhibit 7-3: The Slide Transition task pane

Do it!

D-1:   Adding transition effects

Here's how	Here's why
1 Move to the first slide	If necessary.
Choose **Slide Show**, **Slide Transition...**	The Slide Transition task pane appears.
2 From the Apply to selected slides list, select **Blinds Vertical**	A preview of the effect appears in the slide.
3 Click **Play** as shown	
	To see a preview of the transition in the slide.
4 Under Modify Transition, from the Speed list, select **Medium**	To change the speed at which the transition occurs.
5 Under Advance slide, verify that On mouse click is checked	
Under Advance slide, verify that Automatically after is cleared	
6 From the Sound list, select **Applause**	To apply the specified sound effect to the first slide.
Observe the slide	
	The Transition icon appears below the slide number.
7 Click **Play**	To preview the Blinds Vertical transition and hear the applause.
8 Update the presentation	

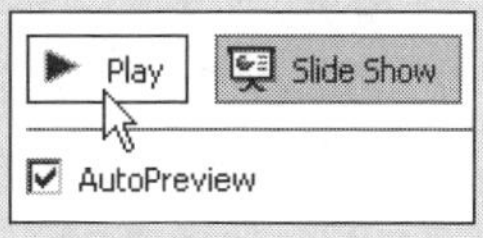

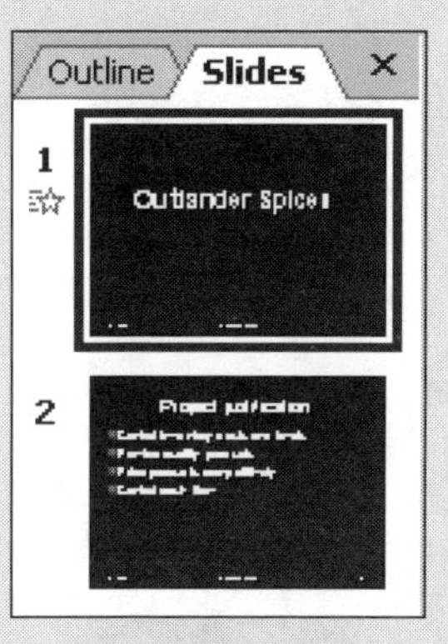

Setting timings for a slide show

Explanation

You can set timings manually for each slide, then run the slide show to review the timings that you have set. You can also record timings automatically as you rehearse the presentation. Timings are useful when you want the audience to spend more time reading a particular slide. You can also use recorded timings for running a slide show in a kiosk or as a continuous background show at a convention or in a store.

To manually set the timing for a slide show:

1 Display the Slide Transition task pane.

2 Under Advance Slide, select both On mouse click and Automatically after.

3 Under Advance Slide, in the box, set the timings between slides by entering the appropriate number of seconds.

4 Click Apply to All Slides.

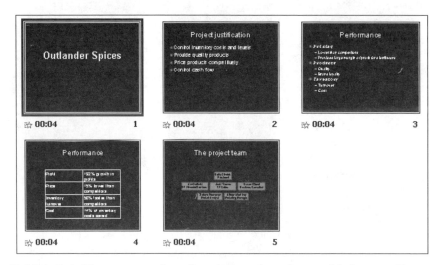

Exhibit 7-4: The presentation after timings have been added manually

Do it!

D-2:   Adding timings to a slide show

Here's how	Here's why
1 Under Advance slide, select **Automatically after**	
2 Under Automatically after, enter **00:04**	`00:04  ⬍`
	To set the timing to four seconds between slides. You can use the spinner controls or your keyboard to enter the time interval.
3 Click **Apply to All Slides**	Apply to All Slides ▶ Play 💷 Slide Show
	To apply the transition effect to all the slides in the presentation. Note that the Transition icon appears below each slide number in the Slides tab.
4 Switch to Slide Sorter view	
	Observe the view	Under each slide, you'll see the Transition icon along with a timing indicator, as shown in Exhibit 7-4.
5 Choose **Slide Show**, **View Show**	To view the slide show.
	View the presentation	You'll see that the slides appear automatically after an interval of 00:04 seconds.
6 Update the presentation	

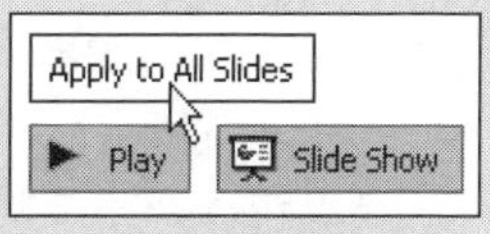

Rehearsing slide show timings

Explanation

You can use the Rehearse Timings feature to finetune your pace before you give a presentation. You can set the timings for your slides before you rehearse, or you can set them automatically while you rehearse. If you set them before you rehearse, you'll find it easier to work in Slide Sorter view where you can see miniature versions of each slide in the presentation. You can use the buttons in the Rehearsal dialog box to pause between slides, restart a slide, and advance to the next slide. PowerPoint keeps track of how long each slide appears and sets the timing accordingly. When you finish your rehearsal, you can accept the timings or you can try again.

To rehearse timings:

1 Choose Slide Show, Rehearse Timings.
2 Click the Next button on the Rehearsal dialog box to move through your presentation.
3 Click Yes to record the timings.
4 Press F5 to view the slide show.

Exhibit 7-5: A part of the slide with the Rehearsal dialog box displayed

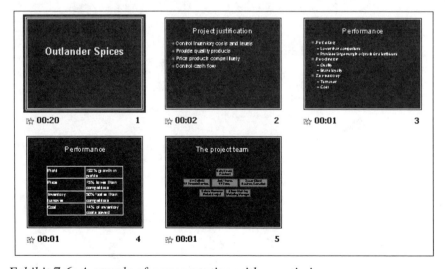

Exhibit 7-6: A sample of a presentation with new timings

Do it!

D-3:   Rehearsing timings

Here's how	Here's why
1 Choose **Slide Show**, **Rehearse Timings**	You might have to click the chevrons to reveal this option.
Observe the screen	You'll see the first slide with the Rehearsal dialog box displayed (as shown in Exhibit 7-5).
2 Click ➡	(In the Rehearsal dialog box.) To move to the next slide.
3 Click ➡ until you reach the end of the presentation	You'll see a message box.
Observe the message box	
	Microsoft PowerPoint ⬚
	ⓘ The total time for the slide show was 0:00:24. Do you want to keep the new slide timings to use when you view the slide show?
	[Yes] [No]
	It displays the total time for the slide show.
4 Click **Yes**	To record the new slide timings.
Observe the window	You'll see that the timing indicators display the new slide timings (as shown in Exhibit 7-6).
5 Press **F5**	To view the slide show.
View the presentation	You'll see that the slides appear automatically at the specified intervals.
6 Update the presentation	

Topic E: Adding speaker notes and footers

Explanation

Each slide can have corresponding notes to help the presenter remember the key points in a presentation. Every slide in your presentation has a *Notes page* that contains a slide image and space for speaker notes. The presenter can use the speaker notes as a reference tool and can also print them to distribute to the audience.

Adding speaker notes

You can add speaker notes in Normal view, or you can choose View, Notes Page. The Notes Master controls the format of the Notes page. It has a Master Object Area that you can format.

To add speaker notes to a slide from within Normal view:

1 Click the Notes pane for the slide to which you want to add speaker notes.
2 Enter the text.
3 View the Notes page.

Do it!

E-1: Adding speaker notes

Here's how	Here's why
1 Click ▣	(The Normal View button is in the lower-left corner of the PowerPoint window.) To switch to Normal view.
Observe the slide	You'll see the first slide.
2 Click the **Outline** tab	
Click in the Notes pane	(It's below the slide.) You'll enter text in this pane.
3 Enter the text as shown	Outlander Spices is a very small, privately held company that provides exotic spices and gourmet foods to restaurants throughout the United States.
4 Move to the fifth slide	(You might need to scroll.) You'll see a slide titled 'The project team."
5 Enter text in the Notes pane as shown	The project team is made up of five internal employees and one outside consultant.
6 Choose **View**, **Notes Page**	To view the slide with the notes.
7 Click the Normal View button	To switch back to Normal view.
8 Update the presentation	

Adding footers to a presentation

Explanation

Footers are found at the bottom of each slide. You can use footers to display information common to the entire presentation, such as the date and time of the presentation, the slide or page number, or the occasion for the presentation. You can also include the company name or copyright information in the footers. You can add similar footers to speaker notes.

To add a footer to a slide:

1 Choose View, Header and Footer.
2 Click the Slide tab (if necessary) and verify that Footer is selected.
3 Enter your text in the Footer text box.
4 Click Apply to All.

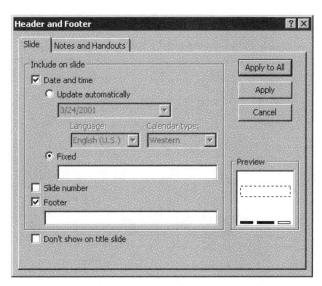

Exhibit 7-7: The Header and Footer dialog box with the Slide tab displayed

Do it!

E-2:   Adding footers to slides

Here's how	Here's why
1 Choose **View**, **Header and Footer...**	To display the Header and Footer dialog box.
Observe the dialog box	You'll see various options, as shown in Exhibit 7-7.
2 Verify that the Slide tab is selected	
3 Under Include on slide, check **Date and time**	If necessary.
4 Select **Update automatically**	To display the current date and time.

5 Check **Slide number**	To display the slide number.
6 Check **Footer**	If necessary.
7 Under Footer, enter **Outlander Spices**	In the text box.
Click **Apply to All**	To apply the Header and Footer settings to all the slides in the presentation.
8 Update the presentation	

Adding footers to speaker notes

Explanation   You might want to include the date and company name on the speaker notes for a presentation. You can add footers to speaker notes by opening the Header and Footer dialog box and clicking the Notes and Handouts tab.

To add footers to speaker notes:

1   Open the Header and Footer dialog box and click the Notes and Handouts tab.
2   Select the ppropriate options.
3   In the Footer text box, enter the text you want to display in the footer.
4   Click Apply to All.

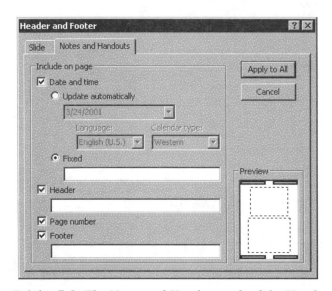

Exhibit 7-8: The Notes and Handouts tab of the Header and Footer dialog box

Do it!   **E-3:   Adding footers to notes**

Here's how	Here's why
1 Open the Header and Footer dialog box	Choose View, Header and Footer.
2 Click the **Notes and Handouts** tab	To display the various options on the tab, as shown in Exhibit 7-8.
3 Under Include on page, check **Date and Time**	If necessary.
4 Select **Update automatically**	To display the current date and time.
5 Clear **Header**	If necessary.
6 Check **Page number**	(If necessary.) To insert page numbers.
7 Check **Footer**	(If necessary.) To display the footer.
8 Under Footer, type **Presentation for Investors**	In the text box.
9 Click **Apply to All**	To apply the new settings to all the notes in the presentation.
10 Choose **View**, **Notes Page**	
Observe the Notes page	You'll see the footer in the lower-left corner of the Notes page.
11 Click the Normal View button	To switch back to Normal view.
12 Update and close the presentation	

Unit summary: Enhancing presentations

Topic A   In this unit, you learned how to create a presentation based on a **design template**. You also learned how to **apply a design template** to an existing presentation and **format slides differently in a single presentation**.

Topic B   Then, you learned about the various components of a **slide master**. You learned how to format the **Master Title Area** and the **Master Object Area**. You saw that you can select and format the Master Object Area by using the **Bulleted tab** of the Bullets and Numbering dialog box.

Topic C   Next, you learned how to **insert a new slide master**, use **multiple slide masters**, and **delete a slide master** from a presentation.

Topic D   Next, you learned how to add **transition effects** to your presentation. You learned how to finetune the pace of your presentation by manually **adding timings** and by using the **Rehearse Timings** option.

Topic E   Finally, you learned how to add **speaker notes** and **footers** to slides. You learned that you can add a footer to a specific slide or to all the slides in a presentation. You learned that you can use speaker notes to provide information to the presenter.

Independent practice activity

1 Open Progress to date.

2 Apply a design template of your choice.

3 Change the font of the Master Title Area to Arial Black.

4 Change the font of the Master Object Area to Arial Narrow.

5 Change the first level bullet style.

6 Save the presentation as **My progress to date**.

7 Add a new slide master of your choice.

8 Apply the new slide master to all the slides.

9 Add transition effects.

10 Rehearse the timings.

11 Add speaker notes to slides 2 and 3.

12 Compare your presentation to Exhibit 7-9. (Your presentation is likely to be different depending on the design template, bullet style, and transition timings you select.)

13 Update and close the presentation.

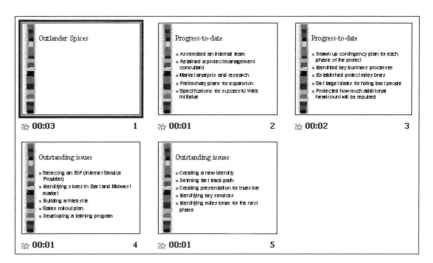

Exhibit 7-9: A sample of the enhanced presentation

Unit 8

Delivering presentations

Unit time: 45 minutes

Complete this unit, and you'll know how to:

A Run a presentation after previewing it and after hiding slides.

B Print an entire presentation, an individual slide, handouts and Notes pages by using the Print dialog box.

C Export a presentation to Microsoft Word.

D Save a presentation for Web delivery, add a link to a presentation, and send a presentation via e-mail.

Topic A: Running presentations

Explanation

After you finish the slides for your presentation, you'll want to run the presentation to see what it looks like. Before you do so, however, it's a good idea to preview it to make sure that the slide order is correct and that you want to include all the slides in the presentation.

Previewing presentations

You can preview a presentation by using *Slide Sorter view*. Slide Sorter view displays a miniature version of each slide in the presentation. You can see all the components on every slide and can make changes to them, if necessary.

Running presentations

After you preview your presentation, you can run it by using *Slide Show view*. Slide Show view displays each slide in the presentation by using the full screen area. You run a slide show beginning with the first slide by choosing Slide Show, View Show or by choosing View, Slide Show. You can also click the Slide Show button at the bottom of the window when the first slide is selected.

Starting a slide show from a specific slide

You can also start a slide show from a specific slide in a presentation. To begin a slide show from a specific slide:

1   In any view, select the slide with which you want to begin.
2   Click the Slide Show button.

Do it!

A-1:   Previewing and running a presentation

Here's how	Here's why
1 Open Presentation	From the current unit folder.
2 Switch to Slide Sorter view	
3 Observe the window	You'll see miniature versions of all the slides.
4 Click 🖵	To switch to Slide Show view.
5 Move to the next slide	(Click the mouse.) You'll see the second slide.
6 Press (PAGE DOWN)	To move to the next slide.
7 Press (PAGE DOWN) until you reach the end of the presentation	To run the entire presentation.
Observe the window	You return to Slide Sorter view.
8 Save the presentation as **My presentation**	

Hiding and unhiding slides

Explanation

When you run a presentation, you might want to hide some slides that aren't required during the slide show. For example, you might not want to give the information contained in a given slide to a particular audience. So, rather than deleting the slide from the presentation, you can hide it during the slide show. To hide a slide, select it and choose Slide Show, Hide Slide or click the Hide Slide button on the Slide Sorter toolbar. The Hide Slide button works as a toggle. When you want to show a hidden slide again, you select that slide and click the Hide Slide button.

Do it!

A-2: Hiding and unhiding slides

Here's how	Here's why
1 Click 🔳	If necessary.
2 Select the Celebration slide	You'll hide this slide.
3 Click 🔳	The Hide Slide button is on the Slide Sorter toolbar.
Observe the slide	The Hide Slide icon appears under the slide. Notice the line drawn through the slide number.
4 Select the first slide	To begin the slide show from the first slide.
5 Click 🔳	You'll run the presentation.
Move through the presentation	You'll see that the Celebration slide doesn't appear in the slide show.
6 Update the presentation	

Topic B: Printing presentations

Explanation

PowerPoint has many options for printing a presentation. You can print an entire presentation or an individual slide. You can also print the Notes pages.

Previewing a presentation in black and white

By default, PowerPoint creates presentations in color. If you want to print the presentation in black and white, you might want to preview it to make sure that all the slides have the correct shades of gray. To preview a presentation in black and white, choose View, Color/Grayscale, Pure, Black and White. To preview a presentation in gray, choose View, Color/Grayscale, Grayscale. You can also use the Color/Grayscale button on the Standard toolbar to switch between color, grayscale, or black and white preview.

Do it!

B-1: Previewing a presentation in black and white

Here's how	Here's why
1 Click 🔳	If necessary.
2 Choose **View, Color/Grayscale, Grayscale**	To view the slides in gray.
Observe the slides	All the colors have changed to gray. Also note the Grayscale View toolbar that appears.
3 Choose **View, Color/Grayscale, Pure Black and White**	To view the slides in black and white.
4 Click **Close Black and White View**	On the Grayscale View toolbar.
Observe the slides	All the colors reappear.
5 Update the presentation	

Printing presentations

Explanation

When you choose File, Print, PowerPoint opens the Print dialog box, as shown in Exhibit 8-1. Here you can choose the printer to which you want to send the presentation. You can also specify a range of slides and the number of copies to print.

Slide formats

You can print slides in a variety of formats. The presentation's page setup determines the *size* and *orientation* of the printed output. In PowerPoint, size refers to the size of the slide on a printed page, while orientation refers to whether the pages are set up as portrait (8.5" × 11") or landscape (11" × 8.5"). The default settings for any new presentation are for an on-screen slide show with landscape orientation. The slide numbering begins with 1. Handouts, outlines, and notes all print in portrait orientation by default. Of course, you can change these settings.

To change the slide size format:

1 Choose File, Page Setup to open the Page Setup dialog box.
2 From the Slides sized for list, select the required format.
3 Under Orientation, select an Orientation (Portrait or Landscape) for the slides and the other components of the presentation.
4 Click OK.

Slide size format options

The following table describes some of the available size format options in the Page Setup dialog box:

Format	Description
On-screen Show	This is the default setting and should be used when designing a presentation you plan to show on-screen. The slides are sized slightly smaller than a standard sheet of paper.
Letter Paper (8.5×11 in)	With this setting you can print the presentation on standard US letter stock (8.5" × 11").
Ledger Paper (11x17 in)	With this setting you can print the presentation on standard US Ledger (11" x 17").
A3 Paper (297×420 mm)	With this setting you can print the presentation on international letter stock (297 mm × 420 mm).
A4 Paper (210×297 mm)	With this setting you can print the presentation on international letter stock (210 mm × 297 mm).
35mm Slides	This setting, which is only slightly smaller than the default, adapts the presentation to 35mm slides.

Format	Description
Overhead	With this setting you can print your slides on overhead transparency stock (8.5" × 11").
Banner	This setting adjusts the slide size to create an 8" × 1" banner when printed.
Custom	With this setting you can adjust the slide size to accommodate special sizing requirements.

Printing overhead transparencies

If you are using a non-color (black-and-white) printer to create overhead transparencies, you should preview the slides in black and white before printing. You can then make any necessary adjustments before printing your presentation directly on overhead transparency stock.

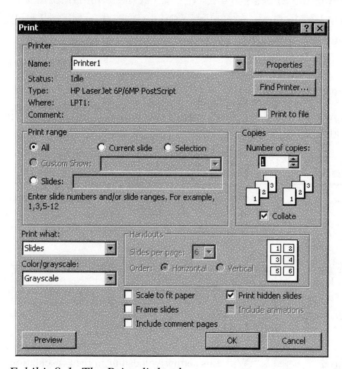

Exhibit 8-1: The Print dialog box

Using the Print button

You can use the Print button to print a presentation without going through the Print dialog box. When you do so, PowerPoint prints the entire active presentation to the current printer by using the default settings.

Do it!

B-2: Printing a presentation

Here's how	Here's why
1 Choose **File**, **Print...**	To display the Print dialog box. It should resemble Exhibit 8-1, although the options in this dialog box differ depending on the kind of printer you use.
2 Observe the Print range options	If you have a multiple slide presentation, you can choose to print a specific range. By default, All is selected.
3 Observe the Copies options	You can print multiple copies, collated or not.
4 Observe the Print what options	You'll see that Slides is selected.
5 Observe the Color/grayscale options	You can print in gray, black and white, or color.
6 Click **Preview**	A preview of how your presentation will look after printing appears in the preview window. The Print dialog box disappears.
Click **Close**	To close the preview window.
7 Click 🖨	(On the Standard toolbar.) To print the entire presentation by using all the current settings.
8 Update the presentation	

Printing individual slides

Explanation

You also have the option of printing only a single slide from a presentation. To do so, select the slide you want to print, open the Print dialog box, and select Current slide (under Print range). You can also specify the number of copies of the selected slide you want to print.

Do it!

B-3: Printing an individual slide

Here's how	Here's why
1 Select the first slide	If necessary.
2 Press ⌈CTRL⌋ +P	This is the shortcut key for the File, Print command.
3 Under Print range, select **Current slide**	You'll print only the first slide.
4 Click **Preview**	To see a preview.
Click **Close**	To close the preview window.
5 Update the presentation	

Print output options

Explanation

PowerPoint provides several print output options. You can print only slides, audience handouts, speaker notes, or a presentation outline. You can use the Print what list in the Print dialog box to specify the type of output you want to create.

Audience handouts

You can create audience handouts for your presentation by using the Print dialog box. You can print these handouts with 2, 3, 4, 6, or 9 slides per page. When you are deciding how many slides to include per page, consider the readability of the handout. If you include too many slides with text, it might be difficult for your audience to read. To print audience handouts:

1 Choose File, Print.
2 From the Print what list, select Handouts.
3 Under Handouts, from the Slides per page list, select the number of slides you want to include on each page.
4 Click OK.

Presentation outlines

You can also print an outline of your presentation. The printed outline will show your content as it appears on your screen in the Outline tab. For example, if your outline is completely collapsed you will see only the slide titles in the outline; if your outline is fully expanded you'll get a printout of everything you see. To print an outline of a presentation:

1 Choose File, Print.
2 From the Print what list, select Outline View.
3 Click OK.

Speaker notes

You can print speaker notes for your presentation as well. Each page of speaker notes includes a small version of the associated slide. This will help you keep track of your progress as you deliver your presentation. To print speaker notes:

1 Choose File, Print.
2 From the Print what list, select Notes Pages.
3 Under Print range, select Slides.
4 In the Slides box, enter the desired slide range. For example, you can print the speaker notes for slides 1, 2, 3, 4, and 7 by entering "1-4, 7."
5 Click OK.

Do it!

B-4:   Printing handouts and notes

Here's how	Here's why
1 Press (CTRL) +**P**	
2 From the Print range options, select **All**	
3 From the Print what list, select **Handouts**	You'll print the handouts for your presentation.
Observe the Handouts options	*Handouts* *Slides per page:* 6 *Order:* Horizontal Vertical [1][2] [3][4] [5][6]
	You can specify how many slides you want printed on a single page. Also note the preview of the horizontal order of the slides.
From the Order options, select **Vertical**	Note the preview of the vertical order of the slides.

4	Click **Preview**	A preview of the handouts appears in the preview window.
	Close the preview window	Click Close.
5	Press `CTRL` +**P**	
6	From the Print what list, select **Notes Pages**	You'll print the speaker notes for your presentation.
7	Click **Preview**	A preview of the Notes page appears in the preview window.
	Close the preview window	Click Close.
8	Update the presentation	

Topic C: Exporting to other formats

Explanation

PowerPoint provides many ways in which you can deliver your presentation. You can deliver it by exporting it to Microsoft Word, and to overhead transparencies.

Exporting to Word

To export a presentation to Microsoft Word, choose File, Send to, Microsoft Word, and then select an appropriate option from the Send to Microsoft Word dialog box, as shown in Exhibit 8-2.

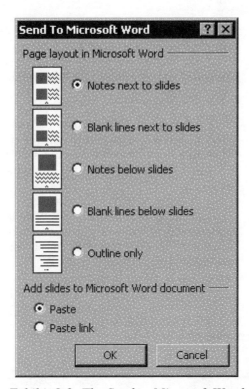

Exhibit 8-2: The Send to Microsoft Word dialog box

The following table explains the various options in this dialog box:

Option	Description
Notes next to slides	Each slide's notes appear next to the slide, on the right, in the Microsoft Word document.
Blank lines next to slides	Blank lines appear next to each slide, on the right, in the Microsoft Word document.
Notes below slides	Each slide's notes appear below the slide in the Microsoft Word document.
Blank lines below slides	Blank lines appear below each slide in the Microsoft Word document.
Outline only	An outline of the entire presentation appears in the Microsoft Word document.
Paste	Embeds your slides in the Microsoft Word document. There's no link between the source presentation file and the destination Microsoft Word document. You can double-click the slides in the Microsoft Word document to use Microsoft PowerPoint to edit them.
Paste link	Inserts your slides in the Microsoft Word document and also creates a link between the source presentation file and the destination Microsoft Word document. The slides get updated each time you open the Microsoft Word document and also whenever the presentation changes.

Do it!

C-1: Exporting to Word

Here's how	Here's why
1 Choose **File**, **Send to**, **Microsoft Word...**	To open the Send to Microsoft Word dialog box.
2 Under Page layout in Microsoft Word, select **Notes below slides**	You'll export the slides along with the notes.
3 Click **OK**	To export the presentation.
Observe the Microsoft Word window	Microsoft Word opens a document containing the slides and notes.
4 Close the Microsoft Word window	You don't need to save changes.

Topic D: Saving presentations for Web delivery

Explanation

By saving your PowerPoint presentation for Web delivery, you can make it available to anyone who has access to the Internet or to your corporate intranet. You can also add links to other presentation files so that the other files can be accessed from the Web.

Saving presentations as Web pages

You can use the File, Save as Web Page command to save a presentation as an HTML document that can be viewed through a Web browser. When you choose this command, PowerPoint displays the Save As dialog box, which contains several options specific to saving Web pages. If you click the Publish button, PowerPoint displays the Publish as Web Page dialog box. This dialog box (shown in Exhibit 8-3) contains Web-specific options for saving your presentation.

The Publish option

When you publish a presentation using the Publish option, others can access your presentation via the Web or another computer to which they have access. You can publish a presentation that has been saved as a .ppt format (the original PowerPoint format) or as a Web page. When you publish a presentation, a copy is saved to the location you specify.

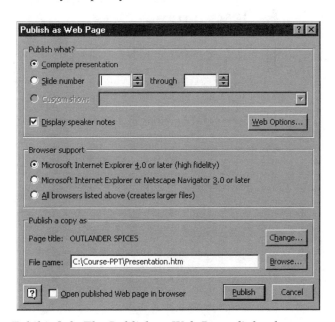

Exhibit 8-3: The Publish as Web Page dialog box

When you open a presentation in Internet Explorer, some additional buttons appear in the browser window. These buttons are specific to PowerPoint presentation Web pages. Exhibit 8-4 shows a published presentation in Internet Explorer.

Exhibit 8-4: A published presentation in Internet Explorer

The table below describes the Internet Explorer buttons that are specific to PowerPoint presentations:

Button	Description
Outline	Works as a toggle that hides or unhides the Outline pane
	Expands or contracts the outline text in the Outline pane
	Displays the previous slide in the presentation
	Displays the next slide in the presentation
	Displays the presentation in Full Screen view
Notes	Toggles between showing and hiding the Notes pane

Do it!

D-1: Saving a presentation as a Web page and publishing it

Here's how	Here's why
1 Choose **File**, **Web Page Preview**	PowerPoint launches Internet Explorer and loads a preview of what the presentation will look like when published as a Web document.
Maximize Internet Explorer	(If necessary.) To view the window in full screen.
2 Close Internet Explorer	Choose File, Close.
3 Choose **File**, **Save As Web Page...**	To display the Save As dialog box.
From the Save in list, select the current unit folder	(If necessary.) It's within the Student Data folder.
4 Click **Publish**	To display the Publish as Web Page dialog box.
Observe the dialog box	You can choose to publish the entire presentation or you can specify a range of slides. You can also add browser support.
5 Edit the File name box as shown	File name: C:\Student Data\Unit_08\Web presentation.htm
6 Check **Open published Web page in browser**	To confirm that your presentation file is published and then opens in a browser.
7 Click **Publish**	To publish the presentation and open it in Internet Explorer.
Maximize Internet Explorer	(If necessary.) Your screen should resemble Exhibit 8-4.
8 Click **Outline**	(In the lower-left corner of the Internet Explorer window.) To hide the Outline pane.
9 Click 🖳	(In the lower-right corner of the Internet Explorer window.) To run the slide show.
Click the mouse	To advance the slides.
10 Close Internet Explorer	
11 Update and close the presentation	

Adding hyperlinks to presentations

Explanation

You can add a *hyperlink* to a presentation to provide direct access to other files. A hyperlink is text or a graphic that has been formatted to include a *Uniform Resource Locator (URL)*. URLs are addresses for files on the Internet. When you click a hyperlink, the file to which the URL points will load in your browser.

To add a hyperlink to a presentation:

1   Select the text where you want the hyperlink to appear.

2   Choose Insert, Hyperlink to display the Insert Hyperlink dialog box.

3   Specify the text you want to include in the link.

4   Specify the file or Web page to which you want the hyperlink to point. You can browse for a file or Web page, or select from recent files, or recently visited Web pages.

5   Click OK.

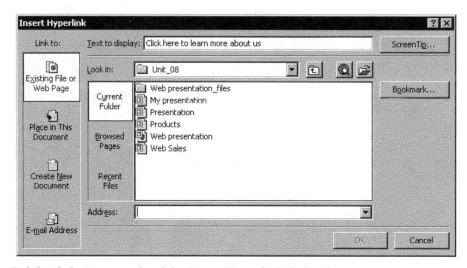

Exhibit 8-5: An example of the Insert Hyperlink dialog box

You can then click the hyperlink to load the specified file in your browser. If you save a presentation containing a hyperlink as a Web page, that link will also work within the Web page.

Do it!

D-2: Adding a hyperlink to a presentation

Here's how	Here's why
1 Open Web sales	(From the current unit folder.) This is a one-slide presentation. You'll add a link to this slide.
2 Select **Click here to learn more about us**	You'll create a hyperlink with this text that points to the Web Presentation file.
3 Choose **Insert**, **Hyperlink…**	To display the Insert Hyperlink dialog box. (It's shown in Exhibit 8-5. However, you'll see a different list of files than the one shown.)
4 Verify that the Text to Display box reads "Click here to learn more about us"	The hyperlink will display this text.
5 Click **Current Folder**	(If necessary.) To display a list of files in the current folder.
Select **Web presentation**	You'll add a link to load the Web presentation page.
Observe the Address box	Address: `Web presentation.htm`
6 Click **OK**	To insert the hyperlink.
7 Choose **File**, **Web Page Preview**	To preview this presentation as a Web page.
Maximize Internet Explorer	
Click the hyperlink	Click here to learn more about us
	To load the Web presentation Web page.
8 Close both the Internet Explorer windows	
9 Save the presentation as **My Web sales**	
Close the presentation	

Sending presentations via e-mail

Explanation

You can send a presentation to someone through e-mail. To do so, you and the recipient must have compatible e-mail programs, and you must both have PowerPoint installed. The exact steps for sending a presentation via e-mail might vary depending on your default e-mail program, but this option works with most standard e-mail programs.

You can choose to send the entire presentation as an attachment or send only the current slide in the body of the message. You can also use the Routing Recipient command to send copies of the presentation to multiple recipients. To send an entire presentation via e-mail:

1 Click the E-mail button on the Standard toolbar. Your default e-mail program will open.

2 Use the To box to address the e-mail message.

3 Click the Send button to send the e-mail message.

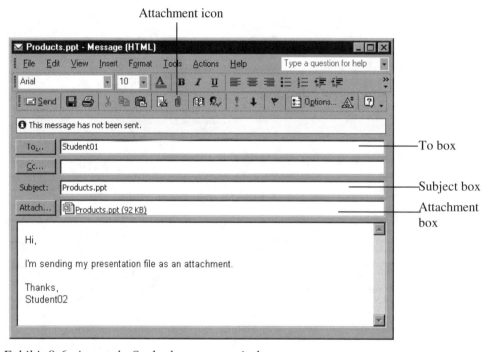

Exhibit 8-6: A sample Outlook message window

Do it!

D-3: Sending a presentation via e-mail

Question	Answer
1 What are the minimum requirements to send a presentation via e-mail?	
2 Which button do you use to open your default e-mail program?	*The E-mail button on the Standard toolbar.*
3 Why do you use the To box?	*To specify the address to which you want to send the presentation.*
4 How do you send copies of the presentation to multiple recipients?	

Unit summary: Delivering presentations

Topic A   In this unit, you learned how to **run a presentation** after **previewing** it. You learned how to **hide** slides that were not required during the slide show.

Topic B   Next, you used the **Print dialog box** to **print** a presentation, a slide, and Notes pages.

Topic C   Then, you learned how to **export** your presentation to **Word**.

Topic D   Finally, you learned how to save your presentation for Web delivery by saving it as a **Web page**. You also learned how to add a **hyperlink** to connect to other Web pages and how to **send a presentation via e-mail**.

Independent practice activity

1 Open Products.

2 Run the presentation.

3 Print the presentation (if you're connected to a printer).

4 Save the presentation file in the current unit folder for Web delivery.

5 Save and publish the presentation in the current unit folder as **Web products.htm**.

6 Switch to Normal view.

7 Add a hyperlink to the text: Click here to learn more about us.

8 Link it to Web presentation.htm.

9 Preview the Web page in Internet Explorer.

10 Click the hyperlink to load the Web presentation Web page.

11 Close Internet Explorer.

12 Close PowerPoint without saving changes.

Appendix A

MOUS exam objectives map

This Appendix covers these additional topics:

A A table of the Comprehensive exam objectives and their locations in the respective courses.

Topic A: Comprehensive exam objectives

Explanation   The following table lists the Microsoft Office User Specialist Core exam objectives and provides a reference to the location of both the conceptual material and the activities that teach each objective.

Objective	Course level	Conceptual information	Supporting activities
Creating presentations from a blank presentation	Basic	Unit 2, Topic A, pp2	A1
Creating presentations using the AutoContent Wizard	Basic	Unit 2, Topic A, p6	A4
Creating presentations using Design templates	Basic	Unit 7, Topic A, pp2-5	A1-A3
Adding slides to presentations	Basic	Unit 2, Topic A, p5	A3
Deleting slides form a presentation	Basic	Unit 2, Topic D, p18	D3
Adding information to the Footer area, Date/Time area, or Number Area of the Slide Master	Advanced	Unit 1, Topic C, pp10-12	C2, C3
Open a Word outline as a presentation	Advanced	Unit 3, Topic B, p9	B2
Adding text to slides	Basic	Unit 2, Topic A, p4	A2
Edit and format text on slides	Basic	Unit 3, Topic A, pp2-4	A1-A3
Creating tables on slides	Basic	Unit 6, Topic A, p2	A1
	Advanced	Unit 4, Topic B, p10-11	B3
Adding ClipArt images to slides	Basic	Unit 5, Topic B, p6-8	B1, B2
Adding charts and bitmap images to slides	Basic	Unit 6, Topic B, pp5-8 Unit 6, Topic C, pp10-14	B1, B2 C1-C3
Adding bitmap graphics to slides or backgrounds	Advanced	Unit 2, Topic D, p17	D1
Creating OfficeArt elements and adding them to slides	Basic	Unit 5, Topic A, p2-4	A1, A2
Applying user-defined formats to tables	Advanced	Unit 4, Topic B, pp8-9	B1, B2
Formatting slides differently in a single presentation	Basic	Unit 7, Topic A, p5	A3

Objective	Course level	Conceptual information	Supporting activities
Modifying presentation templates	Advanced	Unit 1, Topic A, p2 Unit 1, Topic B, pp4-6	A1 B1, B2
Modifying the format of slides independent of other slides	Basic	Unit 7, Topic A, p5	A3
Applying transition effects to a single slide, group of slides, or an entire presentation	Basic	Unit 7, Topic D, p16	D1
Applying more than one design template to presentations	Basic	Unit 7, Topic A, p5	A3
Applying an animation scheme to a single slide, group of slides, or an entire presentation	Advanced	Unit 2, Topic C, pp13-16	C1-C3
Customizing slides	Basic	Unit 7, Topic B, pp7-9	B2, B3
Customizing templates	Advanced	Unit 1, Topic A, p2 Unit 1, Topic B, pp4-6	A1 B1, B2
Creating and managing multiple Slide Masters	Basic	Unit 7, Topic C, pp11-15	C1-C3
Rehearsing presentations	Basic	Unit 7, Topic D, p20	D3
Changing the order of slides in presentations	Basic	Unit 2, Topic D, pp16-17	D1, D2
Changing the layout of individual slides	Advanced	Unit 1, Topic D, p16	D3
Adding hyperlinks to slides	Basic	Unit 8, Topic D, p16	D2
Printing slides	Basic	Unit 8, Topic B, pp5-8	B2, B3
Printing handouts	Basic	Unit 8, Topic B, p8	B4
Printing Speaker Notes	Basic	Unit 8, Topic B, p9	B4
Printing comments pages	Advanced	Unit 5, Topic C, p13	C3
Inserting Excel charts on slides (either as embedded or linked objects)	Advanced	Unit 3, Topic A, pp2-5	A1, A2
Adding sound effects to slides	Advanced	Unit 2, Topic B, p12	B2
Inserting Word tables on slides (either as embedded or linked objects)	Advanced	Unit 3, Topic B, p13	B5

Objective	Course level	Conceptual information	Supporting activities
Saving slide presentations as RTF outlines	Advanced	Unit 3, Topic B, p12	B4
Setting-up presentations for delivery	Advanced	Unit 5, Topic B, pp7-9	B1, B2
Preparing slide shows for delivery	Advanced	Unit 5, Topic B, pp7-9	B1, B2
Running slide shows	Basic	Unit 8, Topic A, p2	A1
Creating folders for storing presentations	Basic	Unit 2, Topic B, p10	B2
Embedding fonts in presentations	Advanced	Unit 6, Topic B, p6	B1
Publishing presentations to the Web (Save as HTML)	Basic	Unit 8, Topic D, pp13-14	D1
Preparing presentation for remote delivery using Pack and Go	Advanced	Unit 6, Topic B, pp6-10	B1-B4
Setting up a review cycle and sending presentations for review	Advanced	Unit 5, Topic C, pp10-11	C1
Reviewing and accepting and rejecting changes from multiple reviewers	Advanced	Unit 5, Topic C, pp12-13	C2, C3
Saving presentations as a web pages (using the Publish option)	Basic	Unit 8, Topic D, pp13-14	D1
Setting-up and scheduling online broadcasts	Advanced	Unit 6, Topic A, pp2-4	A1, A2

PowerPoint 2002: Basic

Course summary

This summary contains information to help you bring the course to a successful conclusion. By using this information, you'll be able to:

A Use the summary text to reinforce what you've learned in class.

B Determine the next course(s) in this series (if any), as well as any other resources that might help you continue to learn about PowerPoint.

Topic A: Course summary

Use the following summary text to reinforce what you've learned in class.

PowerPoint 2002: Basic

Unit 1

In this unit, you learned how to **open** and run a **PowerPoint presentation**, and explore the PowerPoint environment, including **toolbars** and **menus**. You learned about the various **views** PowerPoint provides, PowerPoint's various **help features**, including the **Office Assistant** and **Ask a Question box**. Then, you learned how to find information and help by using the **Web**. Finally, you learned several ways to **close** a presentation and to **close** PowerPoint.

Unit 2

In this unit, you learned how to create a new presentation by using the **File**, **New** command and the **New Presentation task pane**. You also learned how to add slides to your presentation and select different slide layouts from the task pane. Then, you used the **AutoContent Wizard** to create a presentation. Next, you learned how to **save a presentation in a new folder** and **in an existing folder** for the first time by using the **Save As dialog box**. You also learned how to **update** a presentation by using the **Save button**. Next, you learned that the **Outline tab** shows you the information in your presentation by slide and level. You learned how to create slides in this tab and how to **promote** and **demote** text to different levels. Then, you learned how to **rearrange** slides. You saw that this was possible in the Outline tab but easier in Slide Sorter view. Then, you learned how to **delete** slides by using the **Delete key**. Finally, you learned how to **insert slides** from one presentation into another presentation.

Unit 3

In this unit, you learned how to use the **Formatting toolbar** and how to apply bold and italics to text. You learned how to increase the **font size** and change the **font type**. Then, you learned how to use the **Cut**, **Copy**, and **Paste** commands. You also learned about the **Office Clipboard**. Then, you examined the on-screen **ruler**. You saw that you could use the ruler to adjust **indents** and **tabs** in text. Next, you learned how to **align** text. Next, you learned how to use PowerPoint's **spelling checker**. You learned how to choose the correct spelling from a list of suggested words. Finally, you learned how to use **AutoCorrect** and the **Style Checker** to ensure that your presentation was error-free and consistent in style and punctuation.

Unit 4

In this unit, you learned how to create drawing objects by using the **Drawing toolbar**. You also learned how to **resize**, **move**, and **delete** objects. Then, you learned how to add ready-made shapes by using the **AutoShapes** menu on the Drawing toolbar. You also learned how to edit an AutoShape. Next, you learned how to **add text** in objects and then enhance that text by using the Formatting toolbar. You also learned how to draw **text boxes**. Finally, you used the **Fill Color option** to add colors and patterns to objects. You also learned how to **move** a **filled** object and **change** the **color** of a **filled object**.

Unit 5

In this unit, you learned how to **insert WordArt** into a slide. You learned how to **resize**, **move**, and **change** the shape of WordArt by using the various options on the WordArt toolbar. Finally, you learned how to **insert clip art** into a slide by using the **Select Picture dialog box**. You also explored clip art on the Web by selecting the **Clips Online** option.

Unit 6

In this unit, you learned how to **add a table** to your presentation by using the **Title and Table** layout. You also learned how to **add text** to the **table**. Then, you learned how to add a **Microsoft Graph** by using the **Title and Chart** layout, and you enhanced the chart by using the **Chart Options** dialog box. You also learned how to change the chart type by using the **Chart Type** dialog box. Finally, you learned how to **add an organization chart** to a presentation by using the **Title and Diagram or Organization Chart** layout. You also learned how to enhance the organization chart by changing the **color** and **font** of its boxes.

Unit 7

In this unit, you learned how to create a presentation based on a **design template**. You also learned how to **apply a design template** to an existing presentation and **format slides differently in a single presentation**. Then, you learned about the various components of a **slide master**. You learned how to format the **Master Title Area** and the **Master Object Area**. You learned how to select and format the Master Object Area by using the **Bulleted tab** of the Bullets and Numbering dialog box. Then, you learned how to **add** and **apply multiple slide masters** to a single presentation. Next, you learned how to add **transition effects** to your presentation. You learned how to finetune the pace of your presentation by manually **adding timings** and by using the **Rehearse Timings** option. Finally, you learned how to add **speaker notes** and **footers** to slides. You learned that you could add footer to a specific slide or to all the slides in a presentation. And, you learned that you could use speaker notes to provide information to a presenter.

Unit 8

In this unit, you learned how to **run a presentation** after **previewing** it. You learned how to **hide** slides that were not required during the slide show. Next, you used the **Print dialog box** to **print** a presentation, a slide, and Notes pages. Then, you learned how to **export** your presentation to **Word**. Finally, you learned how to save your presentation for Web delivery by saving it as a **Web page**. You also learned how to add a **hyperlink** to connect to other Web pages and how to **send a presentation via e-mail**.

Topic B: Continued learning after class

It's impossible to learn how to use any software effectively in a single day. To get the most out of this class, you should begin working with PowerPoint 2002 to perform real tasks as soon as possible. Course Technology also offers resources for continued learning.

Next course(s) in this series

This is the first course in this series. The next course in the series is:

- PowerPoint 2002: *Advanced*

PowerPoint 2002: Basic

Quick reference

Button	Keystrokes	What It Does
▣		Switches to Normal view
▦		Switches to Slide Sorter view
▤	F5	Runs the slide show
✂	CTRL + **X**	Cuts the selection and places it on the Clipboard
▤	CTRL + **C**	Copies the selection and places it on the Clipboard
▤	CTRL + **V**	Pastes the selection from the Clipboard
▱		Copies the format of the selection and applies it to the following selection
▤		Left-aligns the selection
▤		Center-aligns the selection
▤		Right-aligns the selection
▢		Draws a rectangle
◯		Draws an oval
╲		Draws a line
▤		Draws a text box
▱		Applies the selected fill color to an object
◀		Inserts WordArt in a slide

Button	Keystrokes	What It Does
		Changes the shape of WordArt
		Inserts a new slide master
		Deletes the selected slide master
		Inserts clip art in a slide
		Hides a slide
		Prints a presentation with all default printer settings
	F7	Opens the Spelling dialog box.

Index